Imagine

"Life is pleasant. Death is peaceful.
It's the transition that's troublesome"
                                    Isaac Asimov

A true story

by

Geoffrey Wilding

Dedicated to Lesley Helen

Formerly entitled 'A Death to Die For'

Prologue

Geoff, having been diagnosed with an incurable cancer, takes us on a journey through what he is told will be the last few weeks of his life. We follow his coming to terms with the fatal diagnosis, his preparation for death and efforts to look after those he will leave behind. We are led through the practicalities of putting his affairs in order and coping with the challenges of daily physical care, which are compounded by the need to say proper goodbyes to those closest to him. He shows us how each day he survives the problems and emotions that circumstances dictate.

Developing through the story, Geoff and Helen show how they draw on the strength of their relationship to rise above the tragedy of the situation. They cope with the pending loss and separation by invoking a beautiful strategy: that of tying an even stronger bond between them, which will reach beyond death and ultimately reunite them both.

It is, first and foremost, a compelling love story of two people's strength and resilience as they endure what appear to be insurmountable odds, which are also borne by a family's courage, as they try to help their loved ones deal with events completely beyond their control.

Friday 25ᵗʰ November 2005

I had always liked owning my Mitsubishi Shogun, but the only reason I could warrant having two cars, was to tell anyone who asked me that I needed the four wheel drive for the bad winters we sometimes get. Living, as we do, in a rural location, the roads are usually the last to be cleared of snow, so its extra grip meant that I could still travel to meet clients. It was with some glee therefore, that I listened to the evening weather forecast on the television and heard that we could expect overnight snow.

It was late November and still dark when I got up. There are no street lights where we lived, but peering out of the bedroom window into the grey light of early morning, I could see that we had indeed had a good covering of snow. I started to prepare for the day's trip while my wife Helen, (*her name is actually Lesley Helen, but I always prefer to call her Helen*), had got up and headed to the kitchen to prepare a hot flask of my favourite Heinz tomato soup and some bacon sandwiches. I wanted to take something warm and nourishing with me in case I got stuck in the snow while on my trip into the Welsh hills where I was to meet some new clients. They were after someone to take on the health and safety management of their proposed new housing development.

We said our goodbyes in the warmth of the kitchen, which made the morning air feel even colder as I trudged across the driveway to where the cars were parked. After having released the Shogun from its wintery cocoon and got the engine warmed up, I tentatively, but excitedly, set off. I was like a schoolboy on a great adventure and all the more pleased to see that very few other vehicles had left tyre marks in the overnight snow.

Excluding the odd slip and slide, I managed, without too much difficulty, to drive the sixty or so miles to my destination. Having concluded a successful meeting, I took my leave and started on the way home. At a lay-by high in the hills, I stopped to have the soup and sandwiches that Helen had made. The wonderful snow covered landscape, sparkling in the low winter sunlight, was set out before me. I sat there with the engine running and the heater on and counted my blessings; there are probably only few times in my life when I had been happier than at this moment.

Having finished the soup and sandwiches and aware that the sun would be setting early, I didn't want to arrive home after dark in case I needed to chop some wood for the log burner or clear some snow off the driveway, so I packed things away and set off again. I was probably about half way home when the car phone rang. I had been having difficulties with a client trying to get their Construction Health & Safety application accepted. This was proving to be a bit of a problem because, as with many others who try for this award, they had not done the necessary background work, which meant that the CHAS assessor was picking several holes in their safety management systems.

This was not the first time the application had been rejected and the irate client was on the phone making disparaging remarks about the level of service they had received; so when the phone call ended, and even though I had done my best with the documentation I had been given (the phrase *making a silk purse from a sow's ear* comes to mind), I was extremely annoyed and could feel that my blood pressure was up.

Just then I sneezed. I don't know what caused it, whether it was the rock salt from treating the road, as it came through the heater vents in the dashboard or some dust within the car itself, but it was a very energetic sneeze - the first of three, which is a family trait. My younger brother Andy and I always have to have three sneezes, one has never been enough.

I thought no more about the sneeze, but later the left side of my throat started to feel sore and having recently got over a case of 'man flu', I was rueful that I might have picked up another bug from someone. Just what I needed, I thought to myself, what with my heavy workload and the Christmas break coming up. I consoled myself with the thought that, at least if it started now, I would probably be over it by Christmas and, therefore, I would still be able to go for our annual get together at Colley's Supper Rooms in Swaythling, near Southampton. We had a group of friends with whom we had done this every year for more than twenty years.

However, by the time I arrived home the soreness had abated a little, but it was still there and I mentioned my concerns about the symptoms to Helen, who agreed with me that if it was going to happen then better it started now, so that it would be over and done with for Christmas.

Luckily no snow clearing was necessary and I managed to top up the log baskets without having to chop any wood so I got myself cleaned up for supper. Later in the evening Helen went to her W.I. meeting despite my protestations about the road conditions, but she said that since I had made it home from Wales without any problems she couldn't see any reason why she shouldn't make the short journey to the next village. As I was unable to contest the point any further, she went on her way and I settled down to watch the TV in the warming glow of the wood burner.

I enjoyed a couple of glasses of wine during the evening, but stopped drinking because I had started to get a headache, which, by the time Helen got home, had become a real thumper. So much so that when she accidentally dropped some cutlery on the kitchen floor while emptying the dishwasher, I yelled at her to stop making such a racket, which only increased my discomfort. I seemed to be getting really sensitive to noise and light.

Helen was understandably upset by my outburst, so once I had said sorry for yelling we decided to have an early night. I took some soluble aspirin to try to try and clear the head ache but, by now, I was already starting to have a tickly cough, which seemed further to support my 'another blooming cold' theory.

As the night progressed, my coughing became more of a nuisance and I could see that I was keeping Helen awake. I decided to put on my dressing gown and take a blanket down stairs to the warmth of the lounge. I sat in the high backed armchair and used the wing as a head rest and, to keep out any draft, I wrapped the blanket around my legs. Sitting upright seemed to lessen the coughing and I managed to get some fitful sleep.

Saturday 26th November 2005

The latch on the lounge door gives off quite a click when used and, at about 6.30am, I was woken up by our son, Jim, coming into the room. He had a part time Saturday job packing sports clothes with a local company.

He was surprised to see me in the chair, dressed in my gown with a blanket around my knees and asked if everything was OK with Mum but, by now, my throat felt like it was starting to close over, so in a very croaky voice I managed to assure him that Mum was fine. However I told him that I could be going down with a cold again; he gave me and the armchair a wide berth and hurriedly left for work.

Helen came down around 7.30 and asked me how I was feeling. "Not too bad", I replied, hoarsely. I told her that the cough was getting worse, but, on the plus side I didn't think I had a high temperature, or other cold or flu symptoms and my sore throat had improved, although it now felt like it was closing over, a bit like croup. She smiled and said that I certainly had developed a sexy husky voice overnight.

She asked me if I wanted any breakfast, but I said that I only really felt like having a cup of tea. When I tried to drink the hot tea Helen had made, I had a huge coughing fit. I couldn't swallow the tea, so I tried to retain it in my mouth, but it was hopeless. What with the coughing and gasping for air, I managed to splutter tea through my fingers and all over the kitchen table. This didn't go down too well with Helen, who made a dash for the kitchen sink, where she pulled open the cupboard door and grabbed one of the many bottles of cleansing agents that were stashed there. A period of purposeful squirting accompanied by vigorous wiping then ensued to clear away the offending mess.

Once I had regained some semblance of composure, I decided that it would probably be the best strategy to remove myself from the disaster area and go and have a shave, clean my teeth and have a shower.

However, this too proved to be problematic: the shave, because every time I tried to lift my chin I nearly choked, a problem that became even more of a trial when I tried, with very little success, to clean my teeth. To top things off, the steam from the hot shower started another uncontrollable coughing fit, with much spluttering and copious amounts of snot.

I finally managed to gain a modicum of control during the process of drying and dressing myself, which passed off without too much commotion. But by now, I was starting to feel that there was something definitely wrong with me, so when I went back down to the kitchen I said to Helen that I thought I needed to see a doctor. She knew that I rarely sought medical advice, which must mean that I was starting to worry about what ailed me, so she started to be more concerned herself.

As it was a Saturday we did not have access to our usual local GP surgery, so Helen telephoned the NHS Direct service who informed her that the only place open was the emergency surgery in Hereford, some fifteen miles away.

Helen ensured that I wrapped up warm, with a couple of jumpers, a winter coat, gloves, scarf and a hat, plus the essential box of tissues, which I carried on my lap. We drove, in her car, to Hereford but, being the only surgery open, by the time we got there the reception area was full. Helen found me a seat and I waited while she gave my details to the receptionist. I still kept all my warm clothing on including the hat, but by now my constant coughing was drawing looks from the assembly of 'ill' people, no doubt worried that they might catch whatever I had on top of their own ailments.

Eventually my name was called. I moved toward the examination room as directed where I found that I was in the presence of a male doctor of foreign extraction, possibly Eastern European, with broken English and the typical forthright approach.

Following some general information questions, I was asked to remove my heavy outer clothing. He placed a thermometer in my mouth, but because of the problems I was having with my throat it was very difficult for me to keep it under my tongue or even keep my mouth shut. This brought on another coughing fit and I nearly spat the thermometer straight back into his face, but luckily it just dropped into my hand.

After some prodding of my neck glands he wanted to look down my throat, using a spatula to keep my tongue down. This stopped me being able to swallow and I felt that I was going to drown. I started coughing so much that tears were rolling down my face because my eyes were screwed tight shut. He said "OK" and that he had seen enough and I was relieved that the trial was over. Having completed his examination, he wrote out a prescription for some penicillin capsules. He said I had to take one four times a day and told me that I should make an appointment to see my own GP, as soon as possible, the following week.

The doctor could see that I was struggling to get my outer clothes on again and helped me put my arms into the sleeve of the coat and then handed me my hat which had been resting on his desk. I thanked him and met up with Helen in the waiting room. I showed her the prescription and she went over to the notice board to see where the nearest available dispensing chemist was situated; once she had found the address we left the surgery. You could almost feel the sense of relief from those still waiting who wanted to be free of the guy with the constant cough.

We soon arrived at the chemist. Helen said that I looked exhausted from lack of sleep and the constant coughing, so she took the prescription to get it filled. She said that this would save me having to go out into the cold air, which would probably set me off coughing again.

Fortunately it didn't take long and when she got back to the car I decided that I would start taking the capsules as soon as possible, in the hope that they could begin working on whatever malevolence I had contracted. I found a half used bottle of drinking water in the car, so I took the box of penicillin out of the chemist's bag, removed one of the bubble strips and popped a capsule into my hand, I then placed it in my mouth and took a good sip of water from the bottle. This proved to be a bad move indeed as no sooner had the water hit the back of my throat my whole body seemed to convulse uncontrollably. My body's natural defence against drowning had kicked in causing an involuntary muscle spasm. Unfortunately, the result was that the penicillin capsule was choked up and ricocheted off the dash board into the foot well with water splattering all over the inside of the passenger windscreen.

Helen looked across from the driver's seat, not sure whether she should laugh or not. She said I looked a dreadful sight, with tears rolling down my cheeks and water and other unmentionables streaming from my nose and mouth. Having pulled the car over to the kerb, she took the box of tissues from my lap and started to wipe me down and then turned her attention to cleaning the windscreen and dashboard. We thought it best for me not to try again until we got home. I coughed and coughed so much that by the time we got back I felt really wretched. It was now about 2pm and having hardly slept the previous night and had nothing to eat or drink for nearly 24 hours, I decided it was kill or cure time and told Helen that somehow I just had to try and get one of the penicillin capsules down my throat in the hope that it would start fighting off this dreadful bug.

Having discarded my outdoor clothes onto the back of a kitchen chair, I took the packet of penicillin and placed it on the draining board, I removed another capsule from its bubble strip and leaning over the sink, so as to catch and wayward projectiles, I put it into my mouth and with my finger pushed it as far back along my tongue as I could manage without retching. I took a small, tentative sip of water, but rather than swallow it straight down I twisted my head to the left, stretched my neck out and swallowed all at the same time. It did set me off coughing again, but I could feel that the capsule had gone down my throat and so I felt quite relieved that I had at last started the fight back.

I spent most of the rest of Saturday sat in the wing back chair with a blanket round me; the TV was on, but it was just for background noise really. Helen busied herself with housework. It's a big house and the weekends are the only time she gets to have a good go at it, but every time she passed through the lounge, she would check on me to see that I was comfortable. I mostly just sat and dozed, occasionally getting out of the chair to either go to the loo or put more logs on the wood burner, but all the time I continued to have bouts of coughing

Jim got home from work about mid-afternoon and wanted to know how I was feeling. Helen told him that we had been into Hereford to see the doctor, who had prescribed some tablets for me and I managed to croak that I wasn't too bad, adding that it was probably just a case of man flu. He said that he was glad that we had gone to get it looked at. Helen asked him if he had plans for the evening, he said that he would be going out and went off to his room to have a rest before getting ready.

It must have been about 6pm when I determined to try and have another capsule. I followed the same procedure as before and managed to get another one down my throat and because it proved not to be such an onerous ordeal as the first time, I started to convince myself that things might be improving.

Helen ran through a whole list of food she could prepare for supper, but I said that I really couldn't face anything and just wanted to sit in the chair and let the capsules do their work. So she went and prepared something for her and Jim to eat and after seeing him off and clearing away the supper things, she came and spent the rest of the evening with me in front of the TV, frequently checking that I was OK and asking whether she could get anything to make me more comfortable.

At around 10pm, by using the same technique as earlier, I just about managed to swallow another capsule and deliver a further dose of penicillin to my immune system. This achieved and being absolutely 'knackered', I said to Helen that I wanted to go to bed and try to get some sleep. She also thought this a good idea and said that she was sure that we had a 'V' pillow somewhere in the box room which I could use to prop myself up in bed and, hopefully, help me not to cough so much.

She went off to find it, and by the time I had got ready for bed she arrived triumphantly in the bedroom with the pillow in hand. I got into bed and she helped to make a comfortable pile of pillows that would keep me semi upright. As Jim wasn't home yet she said that she would wait down stairs for him and, as she left the bedroom, she turned the light off so that I could settle down.

Probably because of my state of exhaustion I did manage to get some shut eye, but around midnight, with Jim safely home, Helen came to bed. Although she tried desperately not to disturb me, the movement of the duvet brought me round and set me off coughing again. It just would not stop, so after a while, and to let Helen sleep, I put on my dressing gown and slippers and once again headed back to the chair in the lounge, where I spent another night of fitful sleep.

During the night I tried to take another capsule, but it proved more problematic than before and after the third attempt, which left me doused from the water I had spilled from the glass, I gave it up as a bad job. I got the towel from the front of the Aga, dried myself down and returned to my self-imposed confinement in the wing back chair.

Sunday 27th November 2005

Helen came down stairs about 7.30am, by now my voice was nothing more than a rasping whisper and I was starting to lose feeling in my right arm; this deterioration made us very concerned and so we decided that I couldn't wait to see my own doctor on Monday. Helen got herself ready and then helped me get into the full winter attire as before. She let Jim know where we were going and then we set off back to the NHS Direct surgery in Herefordshire. I was now feeling quite bilious from not eating, so Helen gave me a bowl to carry on my lap in case the car journey made me feel sick.

After another, seemingly interminably long wait, I was finally called to see the Doctor, a different one this time, probably of Middle Eastern extraction. Through my incessant coughing and croupy voice I again tried to communicate the history of my symptoms. This proved to be a difficult task what with my poor voice and the fact that English was not this doctor's first language.

However, things must have looked more serious today, or this doctor had greater experience than the first one, because during the physical examination, he demonstrated to me that he wanted me to stick out my tongue. As I did so his eyes noticeably widened, until the whites looked completely round in their sockets as, unknown to me, my tongue had corkscrewed to the left, owing to the fact that the whole left side had become atrophied and virtually disappeared.

He became unsure, almost agitated about what to do next. He told me to sit in a chair by his desk and then went to the door leading to the waiting room and opened it. Helen, who had been waiting close by, must have looked up or stood up when he opened the door. Realising that she must have been waiting for me, the doctor called her over and they both came into the room and stood by the chair.

He told Helen that she must take me immediately to the A&E department of Hereford Hospital which, in fact, was only a short distance away. If I hadn't felt so rough we could have easily walked to it from the surgery. However Helen and I were now becoming quite worried, the doctor had not really made it clear to us why we needed to go to A&E, so as quickly as we could she helped me to don my hat, winter coat, gloves and scarf and picked up the tissue box plus the NHS issue cardboard spit bowl. We walked in virtual silence to the car, just exchanging worried glances at each other and Helen drove us to the A&E department as instructed. On the way, Helen phoned Jim to let him know that we would not be home anytime soon and that in the meantime he should get himself something to eat.

We soon arrived at the A&E department, but had to wait in a queue at the reception desk to check in and because my voice was now so weak and the coughing so relentless, Helen gave the requested information for me, after which we were told to take a seat. There were several people who were already waiting, but the answers Helen had given must have rung alarm bells behind the scenes because within a few minutes we were unexpectedly called forward to a cubicle, I could almost feel the daggers land between my shoulder blades as we got up and followed the nurse, bypassing those who were still waiting.

The three of us entered the cubicle and the nurse pulled the curtain around the bed, she then asked me to take off my winter outer clothing and sit on the trolley bed. Helen had to help me out of my coat as by now my left arm was quite weak, this alone was enough to make me think that things were definitely getting worse.

After a short while a junior doctor came to examine me; he said that he needed to take my blood pressure and asked if I was on any medication. I explained, with Helen's help, that I was on some tablets for blood pressure but that it was pretty much under control at the moment.

The duty Consultant then arrived and with Helen's help, I again went through the whole history of events and symptoms as they had occurred up until now. He checked my eyes with his pocket torch, the light was very bright which caused me to flinch, next he asked me to stick my tongue out, I did the best I could, he raised an eyebrow and "Hmmm'd". He asked how long had my speech been slurred. Helen looked quizzically at me, because we hadn't realised it was. He put out his right arm and asked me to grip his hand with my left hand and try to push his hand away, but I could hardly move his hand backwards at all. He stood back, with his hands in his pockets, obviously not sure what was happening to me. He said that he would get the junior doctor to take some blood and then come back in a while to check on me again.

The junior doctor reappeared and much to our surprise, rather than having a syringe to take the blood, as we expected, he prepared to insert a cannula into the back of my hand. Helen asked what he was doing, so he explained that, as they might need to take more than one set of bloods, it would be easier.

After about half an hour the consultant came back, he said that having thought about my symptoms, he was concerned that I might have a rare form of Guillain-Barré Syndrome, known as Miller Fisher Syndrome which, unlike GBS, tended to shut down bodily functions from the top down rather than the bottom up. He said that, although it was a rare condition, he had in fact dealt with a woman with similar symptoms in the past couple of weeks and was therefore fairly confident that his diagnosis was correct.

He started to explain to us how he thought things might progress. Helen looked at me worriedly and said "That's what Alan B had a while ago". This increased my concerns considerably, because only about a year previously, a very good friend of mine had been laid up in hospital with GBS. I clearly remembered his wife phoning me to say that I should make a visit as soon as I could because the prognosis was not very good. The visit flashed into my mind. Alan was laid in his hospital bed unable to move, his breathing was being assisted by a ventilator, with food and fluids being administered using a nasogastric tube. His doctors were saying that even if he survived, it could take at least two years for him to get back to health but, even more worryingly, they said that he might face permanent disability.

On reflection, I can see why the consultant might have thought he was on the right track, particularly when you read the description of symptoms below.

'Unlike GBS, MFS causes descending paralysis, i.e. paralysis that begins in the upper body and gradually spreads downward, damage to cranial nerves weakens the eye-muscles, causing double-vision. It also weakens the facial muscles, causing facial sagging and sometimes making speech unintelligible'.

Alarm bells started to ring in my head as all sorts of questions quickly flooded in. If I ended up like Alan, or worse, how were the three of us going to cope with it? What would happen to our home if I could not keep working?…………What if I didn't make it? All the time my body was racked by endless coughing fits, so much so, that my chest and back muscles had started to ache but, then again, I thought, that it might just be another symptom of the illness.

As the consultant finished his explanation of the possible progression of the illness, my head started to spin. Helen caught hold of my left arm as I leant my head into her side. She put her arm around my shoulder and pulled me closer to her. Here at least I was able to glean some warmth and comfort in my imploding world.

The consultant said that it was important that I was admitted straight away for observation and treatment. He said that he would arrange for a porter to come with a wheelchair to take me up to the Admissions Ward and that he would be waiting for us when we got there.

With Helen still holding my hand, the porter wheeled me into the lift and we went to the first floor. As we approached the Admissions Ward, I noticed that the consultant was already there. He had his back to us and was having a heated discussion with some of the staff at the Nurses' Station. As we got closer I heard his voice rise in agitation as he said to them, "If we can't get hold of a spirometer to keep a check on this man's breathing he could die tonight", Helen gripped my hand tightly.

The words had just left his lips when one of the nurses noticed our approach; I saw her eyes widen and her mouth drop open. She grabbed the consultant's jacket sleeve and nodded in my direction. He spun on his heel and looked straight at me, you could tell from the grimace on his face that I was the last person he intended should hear his outburst. His complexion was now ashen as he turned back to the others, with his head bent forward and in a low voice, which I could barely hear, he continued to urge them to locate a spirometer.

We carried on into the admissions ward and as I still had my normal clothing on I was asked to sit in the chair next to one of the beds. It was a typical green faux leather high backed hospital chair, with wooden arms and, just to be able to sit and close my eyes for a second was a great relief, and gave me a chance to gather my thoughts.

I was quickly brought back to the here and now when Helen asked if I was feeling cold because, although I am sure the hospital was warm, just the sheer exhaustion of recent events had caused me to start shivering. She took the blanket from the bed, one of those that looks like an oversize string vest and folded it in half. She asked me to lean forward and placed it across my back and over my shoulders and I slumped back into the chair again.

Helen sat on the edge of the bed next to the chair and we held hands, her face told of the anguish she was going through. I could tell that she was upset and near to tears, not only because of the diagnosis, but also seeing the suffering I was going through at that moment but, not wishing to transfer her own fears to me, she held them back and managed a smile. Her smile always comforts me.

It was now about 3.30pm and I was having to go through the admissions procedure. With Helen's assistance I had answered the several questions put to me by the nurse, who now gave me my first wrist band, with my name clearly written in biro. It was now evident to both Helen and me that I was going to be in hospital for some time so, because we had been on the go since the early morning, I tried to persuade her that it would be best if she went home and got herself something to eat. It would also be an opportunity for her to let the family know what was happening to me.

At first she didn't want to leave, but realising that there was little she could do, even if she stayed, she reluctantly agreed and said that she would put a few things of mine into a bag and bring them back to the hospital later, so kissing me on the forehead we said our goodbyes and she left.

Almost straight away, the consultant came and sat on the edge of the bed. He put his hand on my arm and said that he was sorry that I had overheard his comments outside. However, he wanted to assure me that I would not die tonight but he was still concerned that that they had not been unable to find the portable spirometer. He said he thought that someone must have removed it from the department for a home visit and not brought it back. The trouble was that the only other unit was locked in the Respiratory Medicine Department but frantic efforts were now being made to try and locate a key, and if all else failed, they would get maintenance to break the lock.

By the time Helen got back to the hospital at around 6.30pm, they had managed, by fair means or foul, to obtain a large trolley mounted spirometer and as she walked into the ward, the nurse was using it to take the first of the prescribed half hourly lung capacity assessments. For anyone who has never had to do this, you have to put a piece of cardboard tube about the size of a toilet roll liner into your mouth and try to exhale air from the lungs for as long as possible, all the time having to contend with the constant refrain of "Keep going" "Keep going" "Keep going" from the operator while they watch the paper read out. However, with my constant niggling cough this was proving to be quite a task, which had to be repeated several times.

The senior nurse then arrived at my bedside with ten small glass jars, each one sealed at the top and filled with a clear liquid, she placed them on the over bed table at the foot of the bed. She explained that the consultant had prescribed for me to have an intravenous preparation called Venoglobulin, I beckoned for her to come closer so that I could ask her what it was. She stepped round the side of the bed and brought one of the bottles with her; she held it out and showed me the label on which I read……

'IGIV (human) products have been linked to renal dysfunction, acute renal failure (ARF), osmotic nephritis, and death. Patients predisposed to ARF include those with pre-existing renal insufficiency, diabetes mellitus, age older than 65, volume depletion, sepsis, or paraproteinemia and those receiving known nephrotoxic drugs. In these patients, give drug at minimum rate of infusion feasible. IGIV products containing sucrose accounted for disproportionate share of renal dysfunction and acute renal failure reports

I looked up from reading the label and in between my incessant coughing I managed to ask her what it all meant. She said that it was made from human plasma and had been derived from multiple blood donors. She thought that it probably came from American servicemen, with that she went off to get a wheeled IV stand and infusion pump.

I looked at Helen but didn't know what to say, I certainly wasn't sure that I wanted this stuff in me but, there again, when you have been told that you have a degenerative illness like GBS, which at worst can be fatal, you have to put your trust in the specialists

Helen brought up a chair from another bedside and put it in front of mine, we sat looking at each other and holding hands for a few moments without saying anything. Her look was almost quizzical, as much as to say, "What happens next?" but I had no thoughts in my head that wanted to coalesce into a coherent answer for her.

After a while she released my hand and reached down for the bag of items she had brought with her and showed me its contents. There was my wash kit, a pair of slippers, the current book I was reading (I think it was a *Rebus* story) and my mobile phone with its charger. I don't use pyjamas at home but I have a couple of nightshirts which I keep for cold winter nights and she had brought these along as well.

When the senior nurse returned with the IV stand, she also brought a hospital gown with her, which she placed on the bed. She asked me if I could get undressed and into the gown as she wanted to connect me up to the IV drip as soon as possible and with that she walked away. Helen stood up and moved her chair out of the way, she then pulled the curtains around the bed. In the meantime I struggled to stand up out of my chair and I managed, with her assistance, to get into the gown.

The senior nurse then put her head through the curtain to check that I was in the bed. Satisfied, she came in and I could see that she was carrying a kidney dish with a syringe in it. She moved the over bed table around to the side of the bed and placed one of the pillows onto it. She said that it would be more comfortable for me if my left arm was kept horizontal while the infusion pump was working and proceeded to connect a line into the cannula that was in the back of my hand. She connected the other end to the IVIG bottle and once she was satisfied that everything was in place and properly connected, she switched on the infusion pump.

As the liquid forced its way through the cannula into my vein, there was a sudden excruciating pain in the back of my hand. I screwed my eyes tight shut and took a sharp intake of breath, which started another coughing fit and beads of sweat ran down my temples. The senior nurse moved to the side of the bed and rubbed the veins in my arm, trying to ease the flow. She said that unfortunately the pain had to be expected, but that it should ease as the process settled in. She then reached for the syringe in the kidney dish and gave me an injection of penicillin in my right shoulder. I said to Helen that I was starting to feel a bit like a pin cushion.

For whatever reason, the nurses didn't manage to stick to the 30 minute lung capacity tests and by 8.00pm I had only been tested twice more. However, the lung capacity readout had remained pretty much the same, which seemed to us like a good sign.

Helen was looking exhausted, which was hardly a surprise, considering the day's events. However, she could see that I was now receiving treatment and in the best place, should I take a turn for the worse. We also knew that it would be a waiting game to see if the IVIG had any effect and so we agreed that it made sense for her to go home and, at least try, to get some rest. It was her normal work pattern to be at the hospital for a full day on Mondays, so unless something untoward happened in the night and the hospital phoned her to come in, she would be able to come to work as normal the next day and still be able to keep a check on my progress. I think that, in reality, she just wanted to have something to keep herself busy, while she waited for news.

Helen drew the curtains back, made sure that my clothes were tidied into the bedside locker and then reluctantly, walked out of the ward, blowing a kiss to me at her final departure.

With the curtains now open, it was the first chance I had to notice the other patients in the room. There were seven other beds in the ward, nearly all which were occupied by people in various stages of dozing or sleeping; all of them, like me, no doubt trying to come to terms with the emotional strain of dealing with the symptoms of their own conditions. The only active person was in the bed opposite and to the left of mine.

He called out "Hi!" and said "My name is Ken" and asked how I was coping. I tried to answer him, but my voice was now nothing but a hoarse whisper and in trying to speak it caused me to have another coughing fit, so I acknowledged him with a wave as I reached for the tissues. He gave me a sympathetic smile and said that he had just returned from abroad, where he had picked up a severe chest infection and that he was due to have a chest x-ray in the morning. I nodded my understanding in return, still coughing.

It must have taken more than an hour for the contents of the first bottle of IVIG to be infused. I know, because it was well after Helen had left that the duty nurse while checking my progress found that the first bottle was empty. She said needed to replace it with a full one, but told me, with a concerned frown on her face, that she would have to up the pump rate, because the other nine bottles had to be infused by the morning. She connected the new bottle and adjusted the flow rate but, when she switched the pump back on, the pain was much more severe. It almost felt like the back of my hand would explode and again beads of sweat erupted on my forehead, but I knew that there was nothing I could do other than grit my teeth and endure the pain.

As the evening wore on I decided to try to get into bed, so carefully manoeuvring around the various pieces of equipment, with my arm still laid on the over bed table, I managed to get onto the bed without incident. I tried to lay down, but straight away the incessant coughing started again, so with my arm still on the pillow I carefully worked my way back into the chair. It seemed quite an achievement at the time.

With my free arm I struggled to try and pull the blanket over my shoulders again and by laying my head on the pillow in front of me, next to my arm, I found that the coughing eased at bit and I was able to gain some fitful sleep. However, when I did cough, the blanket would fall off of my shoulders making me feel cold and with only one free hand, it was difficult to pull it back in place.

It was at this time that Ken restored some of my faith in human kindness, when he got off of his own sick bed and walked across the ward to adjust my blanket, so that it would stay in place.

It was a long night. I came to whenever the IVIG bottle had to be changed. Each time the pain would ease when the pump was turned off but immediately return, stomach churningly bad again, when it was switched back on. I had also twice been woken from a fitful sleep and encouraged to huff into the machine. After the second time the night nurse told me, with a smile, that I had successfully overcome the ordeal by spirometer and wheeled it away.

Monday 28th November 2005

I came to again at 6.00am, when the nurse went through my charts during the changeover with her colleague. As I looked around I noticed there was still one more bottle of IVIG to go, which filled me with dismay. I attempted to assess my condition by mentally working through my body bit by bit, but came to the sorry conclusion that I didn't feel any better at all, in fact my hand felt as though a horse had kicked it and I had a tremendous headache as well.

I hadn't eaten anything now for nearly three days and had only managed small amounts of fluid but, strangely, food and drink did not have any meaning for me; I didn't seem to feel the need for either. However, my stomach did feel very watery and every time I coughed I felt that I might throw up. I mentioned this to a nurse, she went and fetched me a couple of grey pressed cardboard vomit bowls to keep by me just in case.

My next introduction to hospital routine was when a nurse came to my bed with a plastic bowl and placed it on the over bed table. I could see that it was half full of water, with a submerged bar of soap and a flannel. She carefully lifted my arm and pillow from the table and laid it on my lap. Using gentle strokes she washed the sweat off of my face and my arms, the cooling effect of the tepid water evaporating off my skin, was the only pleasant sensation I had felt in the last twenty four hours. The nurse finished the task and before taking the bowl away, she reached the comb from my wash bag and ran it through my hair, making me feel a bit more presentable.

Ken walked past the bed and asked if I was feeling any better. I managed to croak out, "Not really", but thanked him very much for helping with the blanket during the night. He said to think nothing of it.

It must have been about 7.45am when Helen came into the ward on her way to starting work. She looked a bit brighter and her warm smile arrived at my bedside long before she did. Leaning over the bed, she gently kissed my forehead and asked how I felt. I couldn't pretend that I was feeling any better than I had when she had left the night before, but I managed to whisper to her that I had, at least, survived the night and apart from my hand hurting and a nauseating headache, I hadn't deteriorated significantly either, although I was becoming concerned about my left arm and shoulder which were noticeably weaker. Helen said that I must tell the consultant when he did his rounds.

I asked how Jim was coping with things. She said she had updated him on what had happened to me so far and that he wanted to come and see me himself. I said that it would probably be best if he came in with her at visiting time. Helen agreed and said that she would come to see me again at her tea break. By then, hopefully, the consultant would have done his rounds and I might have a clearer idea of what was wrong with me and more to the point what could be done about it.

Just after Helen left the ward, the senior nurse arrived at the bottom of my bed with another 10 bottles of IVIG, which she proceeded to put on the over bed table. She saw my expression of incredulity at having to suffer another eight hours of infusion. She explained that, unfortunately, this is what the consultant had prescribed.

So you can imagine, that not having eaten for three days or, showering and shaving for two, on top of which, I now had a very sore hand and stinking headache, I was not in the best frame of mind to receive the consultant. When he eventually arrived with his entourage of junior doctors, they found me still sat in the bedside chair with a blanket over my shoulders, I had a second one draped over my knees and I was resting my left arm on a pillow laid across my lap.

The consultant removed the clipboard from the end of the bed and examined my notes. He discussed my current condition with the others and then asked me how I was feeling. Had I been in top form, he would have received a fairly acerbic reply; however, all I could manage to splutter, was that my hand hurt and that I had a really bad headache which was worrying me and that when the nurse had taken my blood pressure it had been very high, something like 210 over 112. He checked my notes again and said that he was happy that this was only a temporary situation. He then replaced my notes on the end of the bed and the whole group moved on to the next patient. I was completely fazed by this, because I knew that both of my parents and three of my grandparents had all died from suffering a cerebral haemorrhage.

Knowing this, my GP had spent the last three years trying to get my blood pressure under control, he had even sent me to Birmingham for a MRI scan, to check whether I had berry aneurisms in the blood vessels in my head and now the pressure was all over the place. This brought me to such a low ebb that I just gave into my emotions. I started to sob and tears ran down my cheeks. I was still in a state when a young nurse came to do my 'obs'. Seeing me crying, she asked what the problem was. I said, because my voice was weak, I felt that no one was listening to me, or taking any notice of my concern about my blood pressure levels, or more particularly, my headache. I told her about my parents and grandparents, who had died from having cerebral haemorrhages and how this was worrying me a great deal.

By now the consultant and his team had left the ward, so she asked me what she could do to help. I replied that if she could get me something to write with I could send a note to the consultant, which hopefully, might get the message across. She went to the nurse's station and returned with some paper and a pen. She waited while I scribbled a note and then clutching it in her hand, she left the ward to catch up with the consultant.

It's amazing what the written word can achieve, the final bottle of the first batch of IVIG was now empty and was about to be replaced, but when the senior nurse returned, she said that the consultant had now said that I was not to have any more IVIG and that he had now arranged for me to go for a CT scan. The thought of not having to suffer the pain of further infusions scored as one of those little victories, which can brighten your mood no matter how hopeless things seem but, by the time Helen arrived back in the ward, I had become overwhelmed again and through a mixture of sobbing and coughing I told her what had happened. When I had finished I could see the look of concern on her face. She said that it was good that I had managed to send the note to the consultant and asked me if I knew why I was being sent for a CT scan. I said I didn't know, but that hopefully it might throw some light on the situation.

While she was there, a porter arrived with a wheelchair. Helen helped to transfer me from the bedside chair to the wheelchair, then she wrapped me in the two blankets and placed the vomit bowl on my lap. The porter then wheeled me out of the ward and into the corridor leading to the same lift we had used the day before. Helen walked alongside us and held my hand until we stopped at the lift doors. She said that she would come back at lunch time to see how things had gone.

The air was cooler in the ground floor corridor, probably from the opening and closing of the outside doors. There were lots of people, some visiting and others on duty, they were moving purposely about, going this way and that. The porter tried to chat to me but, because of my lack of voice I could not reply, so we remained silent on the journey to the radiology department. When we got there, the porter parked the chair next to a wall and gave my notes to one of the assistants. She came across to me and asked my name and checked my wrist band, after which she left me sitting there and disappeared through a door opposite.

It wasn't long before she reappeared and wheeled me into the scanner room. I had undergone CT scans before and so I wasn't fazed by the sight of the large white vertical doughnut set at the end of the bed that was situated in the middle of what looked like a fairly small room, however I did remember the claustrophobic feeling of being inside the scanner.

A disembodied voice called my name over a speaker and I turned to face a small glass panel in the wall at the foot of the bed. A lady, who looked quite green behind the glass, leaned forward and spoke into a microphone. She introduced herself as the radiographer and then explained what was about to happen. The assistant helped me from the wheelchair onto the bed and covered me over with the blankets, to keep me warm, in the process I managed to explain to her that I might start coughing if I had to lay on my back for any time, because of the problem with my throat. She smiled and said that I should try my best to keep still but, if I couldn't cope I should raise my arm and she would push the button to make the table slide out of the scanner. The radiographer said that the table would move slowly, so that my head and shoulders would slide into the centre of the doughnut. She would then start the machine which would continue for about 15 minutes.

As my head passed into the machine, I had this uncontrollable sensation of drowning and as I couldn't move my head, I panicked and raised my arm, waving it agitatedly. Almost immediately, the sliding table reversed direction and in my haste to sit up, I banged my forehead on the outer edge of the machine and started to cough violently. The assistant rushed forward with the vomit bowl and paper towels but, after a while, the urge to cough subsided and the radiographer repeated the process so that I was once again set in motion into the scanner.

Unless you have had a scan, I don't think that you can appreciate how closed in you feel and the level of noise generated by the scanning head as it does its work; to call it a rotating loud hum is not nearly a close enough description.

The second run proved more successful, I found that by swallowing frequently I could manage to stay still enough for the scan to proceed. It was a great relief when the scanner stopped and the voice from behind the green glass said "All done". The table slid out of the scanner and the assistant helped me to get off of the table and back into the wheelchair. She then wrapped me in the blankets again and perched the vomit bowl on my lap. Satisfied that I was now in the same condition as when she found me, she wheeled out of the room and parked me against the opposite wall. She then said a cheery goodbye, turned around and disappeared back into the scanner room. By now, I was starting to feel quite chilled and was very pleased to see the porter coming along the corridor towards me to take me back to the ward.

En route to the ward we passed by the discharge lounge, where Ken was stood in the doorway. When he saw me, he smiled and gave a 'thumbs up' sign, but as I knew that things had not improved since the last time I had seen him, I gave him a 'thumbs down' sign in return. His smile changed to a quizzical expression but the porter kept going, so there was no time to stop and say what had been going on.

It must have been lunch time when I got back to the ward. Helen was already there waiting for me to return and helped me to transfer from the wheelchair back into the bedside chair. She asked me how things were going and I managed to whisper to her what happened during the CT scan, but told her that I was still no nearer finding out what the problem was. She sat on the edge of the bed and took hold of my hand unable to hide her look of disappointment at this news so, to try and lift her spirits, I told her that I was feeling buoyed up because at least I didn't feel any worse, which I'm sure would have been the case if I did have the Miller Fisher Syndrome thing.

The food trolley went by and one of the catering staff came across and asked what I would like to eat. Helen told her that I couldn't swallow anything because I had a throat problem; the lady tutted and said that she was surprised that the nursing staff hadn't put a NIL BY MOUTH notice over the bed. Helen spent the best part of an hour with me, trying to keep the conversation as upbeat as possible.

Helen was just about to leave when a nurse came over and said, that after lunch, I was going to be sent to the Ear Nose & Throat Department as the consultant hoped that their investigation might give a clue as to why I continued to cough so much. Helen smiled at me and said she was pleased that things were happening and surely it could only help towards finding a diagnosis. She seemed that bit happier as she left to go back to work.

About 2.00pm a different porter arrived with a wheelchair and after another chair transfer, complete with blankets and vomit bowl, we headed off, this time in the direction of the ENT department.

The porter left me parked in the waiting area and handed my notes over to the nurse as before. Unlike my previous excursion to the scanner room, this time I was sitting in a public area, but being dressed only in a bed gown and blankets I felt a bit exposed, particularly when everyone else was in their normal day clothes, so I was pleased when my name was called when an examination room became free. The nurse pushed the chair towards the open door. People looked at me, the queue jumper, and I could feel a sense of umbrage from those who were still waiting, probably already past their appointment time. It was much like I had felt in the A&E Department the day before. I thought, "My God! Was that only yesterday?" So much seemed to have happened.

I was wheeled into a small room, the normal examination chair had been moved to one side so that the wheelchair could be positioned next to the desk. I really couldn't be sure where the consultant hailed from but in a broad, possibly Asian accent, he checked my name and wrist band and asked me what the problem was. This surprised me, as I assumed it must have all been written down in the notes. However, I managed to whisper to him the series of events up to now. After having to repeat a couple of my responses for clarification, the consultant nodded his understanding and then said that he wanted to have a look down my throat.

First, he strapped on a reflector light onto his head and then, leaning forward, he asked me to open my mouth, wide. I could see his left eyebrow arch the second he saw my deformed tongue, then taking a spatula from a kidney dish on his desk he tried to press down on my tongue. This was definitely not the best thing to have done. I was immediately convulsed by an involuntary retching movement, my head flew forward at speed, causing my forehead to collide with his head light and had he not reacted quickly and removed the spatula, I'm sure that I would have swallowed the spatula and half of his forearm. He threw himself back into his chair and shouted for a nurse, who on entering the room and seeing the mayhem, rushed to the dispenser on the wall, where she grabbed a handful of paper towels and started to wipe me down.

Having thrown the spatula into the waste bin, the consultant got up and went to the sink to wash his hands, while in the meantime, with the assistance of the nurse, I managed to stop coughing and compose myself again. The consultant stood at the sink, staring at the wall in thought, all the time washing and then wiping his hands. He turned, and seeing that normal order had finally been restored, walked back to his chair. He sat down again and said that he wanted to pass an endoscope up my nose so that he could have a look at my larynx, however, before putting the endoscope up my nose, it would be necessary to anaesthetise the nasal cavity and with that he took a small bottle with a long thin nozzle from his desk and sprayed some liquid up both my nostrils.

Well you can imagine that as soon as the cooling liquid hit the back of my nose, the coughing and spluttering started all over again, but fortuitously, this time, the nurse was on hand to deal with the ejected bodily fluids. I was surprised to find that the anaesthetic tasted strongly, but not unpleasantly, of bananas. It quickly took effect and things calmed down once more.

The ENT consultant brought his chair close up in front of me. He asked me to sit back, with my head tilted back slightly; he then asked the nurse to hold my head still from behind. I could see, by peering down the sides of my nose that, he coated a thin black tube with a lubricant gel. He leaned forward and at first tried to gently insert the tube up my right nostril, after a couple of failed attempts he concluded that he would have to try my left nostril. This proved successful and as he started to push the tube up my left nostril, he could watch the progress of the tube on a computer screen, which was positioned on the desk somewhere behind my left shoulder. I could feel the movement of the tube in my nose and throat, but there was no real discomfort and he soon stopped once he could see what he wanted to.

After a few "Mmms" from the consultant, he asked me to try to say Eeeee, he said "Again" and then "Again". I tried my best, but it sounded more like I was just trying to clear my throat. Afterwards he emitted another 'Mmm'. He turned from the screen and looked intently at me again, he said that my left larynx seemed to be frozen and, because it did not move to close with my right larynx, I could not make the usual sounds with my vocal cords and this was also the reason for me coughing all of the time, because my inability to close my larynx properly meant that mucus was getting into my trachea. He then surprised me by asking me whether I wanted to have a look.

I had not looked inside my own body before and I wasn't sure that I wanted to now but my curiosity quickly got the better of me and I gave a slight nod. The nurse let go of my head and the consultant moved my wheelchair so that I could see the screen. How interesting. The whole screen was a mass of different colours from pink through red to purple, in the centre of the screen was what appeared at triangular shape with a slightly curved bottom and two sloping sides both of which were partly edged in white. The consultant explained that the white edges were my vocal cords, he then asked me to try and say 'Eeeee' again, as I did so it was clear for me to see that the right hand larynx was vibrating and bending towards the middle, while the left larynx was completely motionless.

He turned me to face him again and then slowly extracted the tube from my nose, the nurse was ever-present with paper towels in hand to wipe away the excess gel. The consultant wrote some notes into my file which he handed to the nurse who then wheeled me back out into the waiting area.

To my relief, the porter was already in place to take me back to the ward and as we made our way through the bustle of the hospital corridors, I started to feel a bit more positive, particularly now that I had seen for myself what was causing my incessant coughing and speaking problems. After all, I had always been a practically minded person and was confident that once a problem was understood, it should be able to be solved.

I got back to the ward and after being offloaded I decided that I would change into one of my nightshirts. I wanted to be a bit more respectable before I saw Helen again. I pulled the curtain around the bed with my good arm and then proceeded, with some difficulty, to remove the hospital gown and struggled into my nightshirt. Then once done, I opened the curtains and got onto the bed under the top cover.

Before Helen went home to sort out Jim's evening meal, she popped in to see me. With my quiet voice I managed to give her the gist of the afternoon's events in the ENT department and how I had actually seen my larynx on the computer monitor. I explained to her, that it was now quite clear to me why I was unable speak properly and couldn't help but cough all the time. She said that she was pleased to see how encouraged I seemed to be by what I had seen and that, like me, she felt much more confident that having identified the problem positive steps could now be taken to deal with it.

After Helen had left the ward, the consultant came to see me. He said that because my breathing had remained stable and I had no further symptoms of Miller Fisher Syndrome, it had been decided by the team, not to proceed with anymore IVIG treatment, at least until the results of the CT scan were known the next day.

This added to my already improved optimism that things were getting better, so when Helen and Jim came back to the hospital for visiting time I was in a much more pleasant frame of mind. We spent the time talking and generally bolstering each other against the recent events and when it came time for them to leave, all of us felt some progress had been achieved and that, hopefully, the results of the CT scan would give a better insight into a way forward.

With goodbyes over and, as I did not have to undergo any more IVIG treatment, I got properly into the bed. The nurse came and piled up my pillows, so that I was almost in a sitting position and like this, I was able to doze. Unfortunately, each time I fell into a more deep sleep, my head would roll back and the coughing would start again.

After this had happened several times, I decided that I might have more success at sleeping, by doing what I had done the previous night, so I transferred back into the bedside chair. I managed to pull the over bed table towards me and put the pillow on it. Laying prostrate on the pillow, I managed a period of intermittent slumber.

Tuesday 29th November 2005

The fact that I was able to walk about, classified me as 'self-caring' and therefore I was expected to take care of my daily ablutions but, to be honest, I was so tired that I couldn't have cared less. It wasn't until Helen came in, at about 10.30am, that I was persuaded to have a shave and a shower and with her help, I shuffled into the bathroom at the end of the ward.

I did manage a one handed wet shave, of sorts, but showering proved to be a bit more problematic. This was because that to enable me to wash around my left side, I had to slap the hand of my, by now, nearly lifeless left arm, onto the shower wall with my right arm and let it stick there until I was finished. Helen tenderly washed my back and helped me to dry myself and, by the time I had finished, I have to admit that I did feel a bit brighter and probably smelled a bit fresher too, particularly when dressed in my clean clothes.

In comparison to what had happened over the past few days, the next couple of hours passed by pretty uneventfully. Helen and I made small talk, all the time, desperately, trying to avoid the main issue, while the nurses and cleaners busily carried out their daily routines; but as I lay on the bed, with Helen sat in the chair at my side, the previous night's lack of sleep caused a general weariness to come over me. I said to her that I really didn't want her to leave but I had to try and get some rest. She said in that case she might as well go on to work, but before she left, she helped me to adjust the pillows so that I could doze for a while.

It must have been about 3.30pm when the consultant came back to the ward. He headed straight for my bed and pulled the curtains closed behind him. I assumed that I was going to be examined again. I could not have been further from the truth and in no way prepared for what was to come.

The consultant stood next to the bed with his hands dropped in front of him, holding onto some papers, he looked very sombre and said, in a worryingly solemn tone, that he had just received the results of the CT scan and the ENT consultant's report. He said that unfortunately the news was not good, I asked him to carry on no matter how bad the news was.

He did a little throat clearing cough before he started to speak and said that, the CT scan had shown a shadow at the edge of, and just below, the left hand side of my skull. This, on top of what was thought to be nerve damage to my throat and tongue, as reported by the ENT consultant, plus having seen from my records that about a year ago I had undergone surgery to have a melanoma removed from my lower left leg had, after a great deal of consideration, led him and his colleagues to the opinion that, probably, a rogue cancer cell from the site of that operation had travelled around my body and lodged on my brain stem, where it was now multiplying. This apparently malignant tumour was the most likely cause of the damage to my nerves, which had resulted in my partial paralysis. It was as though the words had taken all the wind out of him, causing his previously upright frame to slump visibly.

As he finished speaking, it was as if a lightning storm had just gone off in my head. I could feel the blood drain away from my face and a cold clammy feeling made me shudder. What had he said …….. tumour …….. brain stem……. what was he talking about? All I could do was sit and stare at my feet.

The consultant, having revived a bit, started to speak again. I could hear him, but it was as though he had moved far away from me. He continued by saying that the level of my paralysis meant that the cancer was now well established, it could not be operated on and that it would lead to a fatal outcome. However, he said that with treatment, such as chemotherapy or radiotherapy, I might live for up to three months. He finished by saying that, unfortunately, it did seem to be an aggressive malignant tumour and was sorry that he could not offer any better prognosis. He came closer and put his hand on my shoulder, he asked me if I had understood what he had said.

I nodded, absently. I had understood the words, but just could not comprehend the meaning ………. What had he said? ………I was going to die in three months, or possibly sooner, from some unseen globule of matter destroying the nerves in my neck. This was such a surreal statement to me that a picture of a 'Pacman' flashed into my mind. It was chewing away at the nerves in my neck which seemed to be made of intertwined spaghetti.

All kinds of thoughts started crashing into my consciousness. I couldn't stop them; it was as though my inner self was dashing around, looking in every corner of my mind for some place to hide away from this awful truth; everything seemed to be going on at a hundred miles an hour. I don't know how long it took, it seemed a long time, but was probably only a few seconds, when I eventually managed to gain some control and looked up into his face. This was the man who, only the day before, had assured me that I wasn't going to die and now he was telling me that I had less than three months to live. He looked sad.

All I could manage to say to him, was that I needed to see my wife. The consultant knew that Helen worked at the hospital and said the he would go to get her himself. However, for a brief moment he seemed transfixed to the spot, unsure if he should leave me but then, having come to a decision, he briskly stepped outside the curtains and called for a nurse to come and be with me, while he went to find Helen.

I was in a daze, I had no concept of time as I sat there, slumped on the bed, with tears running down my face. All I wanted was my Helen to come and make things better even though I knew that she couldn't. The nurse stood resolutely by the bed, but it didn't really register with me what she was doing or anything she said. My eyes would not focus, my vision was a blurred by tears and I had a sense of falling, deep inside myself, trying to make sense of all this madness.

To me, the only certainties in life are death and the tax man and my motto has always been, 'Live life to the full'. I had been very lucky, mine had been a good life. I had always had a roof over my head and good food on the table. I had never had to go to war (*although I got pretty close in June 1967*) and there had always been someone to love me and I had always said, if asked, that when the Great Reaper came to call he wouldn't get any complaint from me.

But now, here it was, the end was probably less than three months away and my head was full of questions. What was it going to be like? Would it be painful? Would I be aware of it coming? Would there be a bright shining light at the end of a tunnel? Would I see my son and parents again? A cold shudder of panic set in as my thoughts switched to: How I could get Helen through it all and whether I had I left her with the financial where withal, so that she could make a future for herself. I wondered what effect it might have on Jim's 'A' level results and whether he might be able to get a dispensation because his Dad had died. My mind was whirring so much, I could almost feel the cogs going round. However, in the end, the thing that worried me the most was whether I would be able to retain some dignity on this final journey, or end up just a snivelling wreck.

Just then, through the blur, I saw the movement of someone coming towards me. It was Helen, and as she got closer my eyes managed to focus more clearly on her. From the dark streaks on her blue tunic top, it was obvious that she had been crying. A ball of tissues in her right hand was pressed tightly against her upper lip and her eyes were brim full of crystal clear liquid. As she got close to the bed, she leaned forward to reach for my hand which let her pent up tears fall silently on the bed cover in front of me.

Through quivering lips, she managed to utter, 'My poor darling' and place her arm around my shoulder so that she could draw herself towards me. Our foreheads touched and the tears flowed freely from us both. I reached out with my good arm and tried to pull her closer, in an effort to give her some reassurance, but there was none to be had and so we stayed like this, lost in each other, while the consultant and the nurse looked on.

After a short while we pulled apart, Helen dabbed at her eyes with the now damp ball of tissues and then reached forward, to wipe the tears from my cheeks. The consultant could see that we had steadied ourselves and he came round the bed to stand at the side of us. He said in a quiet voice that he knew there was little that he could say which would help us at this time but, if we had any questions at all, that he would try to answer them. Helen replied for both of us when she said that, at the moment, all we wanted was to be together, on our own. He nodded his understanding and together with the nurse, turned and left, pulling the curtains closed behind them.

Now on our own, Helen and I just looked at each other for a moment and then I asked her what she had been told. She explained what the consultant had said, but to my bewilderment, he had told her that it was unlikely that I would make it to Christmas. I was stunned, I could hardly believe that in such a short space of time, my already much reduced lifespan had been reduced even further by two months.

Helen moved closer, she put her arms around me under my arms. Using my right arm, I moved my paralysed left arm onto her shoulder and then reached around her so that I could grab my left hand and pull her tightly to me. Helen's head lay on my chest, just under my chin and I could feel her sobbing; my eyes filled with tears in response, while all the time I was doing little throat clearing coughs, desperate not to have a coughing fit which would disturb this moment.

I don't know how much time passed, but eventually the consultant and the nurse reappeared inside the curtains. We reluctantly released our embrace and Helen wiped her eyes again and got off of the bed. He said that I would be moved from the admissions ward to a medical ward along the corridor, so Helen started to collect all of my belongings from the bedside locker, while the nurse assisted me out of the bed and helped me to put on the hospital towelling slippers and a gown.

The nurse then asked me if I felt that I could walk the few paces to the other ward or whether I would need a wheelchair. I was now standing and, although a little fuzzy, felt that could still manage to put one foot in front of the other, so I smiled at her and said that I would walk. However, it proved to be more of a shuffle than a walk and so this little, slow moving knot of people, led by the consultant, with me and Helen side by side, her arms full of my possessions and the nurse following on behind, gradually covered the short distance to the medical ward.

It was about 3.30pm when I was shown to my new bed, well not exactly a new bed, it was more of a sad old bed, which seemed to droop down at one corner and not at all like the other beds which I had passed on the way, it looked very much like I felt, old and broken.

The nurse helped me to sit on the edge of the bed, after which the consultant asked her, if she would please go and fetch an 'obs' station, so that he could check my blood pressure. He also said that someone would come and connect a saline drip to stop me dehydrating. All the time he was telling me this, Helen, trying desperately not to have to think about what was happening, busied herself arranging and then rearranging my bits and pieces in the bedside locker. It was only when she was happy that everything was properly stowed away that she came round and sat on the bed beside me.

Helen reached out and gently took hold of my hand and, although bravely trying to smile in order to comfort me, her tear filled eyes showed the real turmoil that was going on inside her. She said, although she didn't want to leave, Jim would be getting home from college soon and she needed to sit down and explain to him what we had been told by the consultant. She stood up and handed me my mobile phone and said that I should call her immediately if I needed her to get back to the hospital but that, in any case, she would be back later with Jim at visiting time. After a tearful goodbye she walked out of the ward and it was the first of many times to come that I wondered if I would ever see her again.

I had calmed down by the time the nurse came to connect the saline drip. I explained to her, as best I could, about my coughing and need to be upright, so she agreed that it would be better if I kept my gown on so that I could sit in the chair next to the bed. When she had finished fitting the drip into the cannula I was fully able to take in my surroundings for the first time.

I remember it as a six bed ward. In the bed opposite, an elderly man, who looked emaciated and unaware of where he was, kept calling out in a strained and pitiful way. In the bed next to me the occupant was laying on his side with his back to me and had the bedcovers pulled high so that only a tuft of hair was visible on the pillow. My attention was suddenly drawn to the far end of the room when a nurse entered the ward. She was responding to an alarm that had been set off by the occupant in the bed nearest the door. I can't really recall the occupants of the other two beds.

As I watched the goings on another nurse approached and said that the consultant had requested that I complete a swallow test. In her hands she was carrying a small tray, which held a spoon and a small jar of jam and, after explaining the process, the nurse took the lid off of the jar and took a small quantity of jam onto the spoon. She then asked me to open my mouth and try to suck the jam off of the spoon and swallow it.

You would think that not having eaten anything for so long I would have been ravenous for anything that passed my lips. However whether my condition had altered my taste buds or it was just the jam I don't know, but it tasted horrible and it seemed to take forever to slide down my throat. Anyway, somehow I managed it and so, eventually, before she left she was able to record in my notes that a successful swallow had occurred.

With the nurse gone and the commotion at the end of the ward dealt with, I just wanted close myself off from everything around me. I stood up, took a deep breath and remembering to wheel the drip stand around with me, I drew the curtains and then sat down on the sagging corner of the bed. Now, for the first time since the shock of the news of my impending death, I felt completely on my own and the reality of my situation started to bear down on me.

Sitting in my cocoon of loneliness, I could hear the noises of the ward going on outside my tiny curtained enclosure. People were talking and moving about; there was the distant clatter of trolleys interspersed with the regular plaintive cry from the old chap opposite. Occasionally, my cocoon of loneliness was broken when one of the nurses would poke their head through the curtains to ask how I was getting on. I acknowledged their concern but could only manage a slow, silent shake of my bowed head in response.

I reached for my mobile and, because it was almost impossible for me to make myself heard over the phone, I sent a text to my younger brother, Andy. I don't like predictive text so I input the following in full, "Dear Andy, I'm in hospital, things are worse than first thought, please come urgently. Geoff"

Within a matter of seconds I got a reply phone call from him wanting to know what was going on, in a rasping voice and in between fits of coughing, I managed to give him the gist of what had happened and that I needed to see him as soon as he could make it. He said that he would be leaving work soon and after going home to let his wife, Sue, know what was happening he would come straight from Fareham to the hospital. He reckoned it would take him about two and a half hours.

Huddled in my own small world gave me the opportunity to think and the realisation slowly dawned on me that I had to make a decision, probably the most important decision left for me to make and I knew, deep down, that I would have to do it before Andy arrived. It had become clear to me that there was a choice to be made: whether I could be strong for those around me or whether my Taurean tenacity would dissolve into a drawn out recriminatory, blame the world for my ills, session as I awaited my departure. It is for others to say which I achieved; all I knew for sure was that I wanted to die with dignity and I think that it was this determination which set the course for the following days and weeks.

By now time had moved on and I was still sat on the bed in my self-imposed confinement when there was the rustling of someone trying to find the gap in the curtain, then Helen appeared in my world again, this time with Jim at her side. Her warm smile comforted me, but I could see from Jim's expression that the leap in thought process from Dad who was ill to Dad who was dying had taken a lot out of him, his eyes were puffy and ringed in red.

Jim, not sure what to say or do, came and sat on the bed next to me, while Helen carefully worked her way around the stand and drip feed and sat in the chair facing us both. She gently took hold of my left hand which had the cannula in it and I put my right arm around Jim's shoulders, he said the phrase that I would hear many times, "I don't know what to say". How could anyone under such circumstances? Then he said, "I love you Dad" and with that we all dissolved into tears.

Helen grabbed a handful of tissues from the box on the bedside locker and handed them around. We all blew our noses in unison and then, through the tears, the strangest thing happened, we all started to chuckle at the silliness of the noise. I put my arm around Jim again and pulled him tight. I said, "I love you too son" and with that, Helen squeezed my left hand and smiled at the unity of it and just for a moment our spirits were uplifted. However, the weight of the situation bore down on us again and the smiles quickly faded, although for myself, I did feel the humour of the sneezes had caused a release of tension in me, lifting the black fog which had enveloped me for the past hour or so.

Jim asked how I was feeling. With the best smile I could muster, I managed to wheeze to him that it wasn't too bad at the moment, apart from not being able to speak, the frequent coughing fits and my gammy left arm. Helen started to unpack the things she had brought with her which she thought I might need. There was some underwear, a pair of lightweight loose fitting trousers, my slippers and a couple of sport shirts and while she arranged the items in the bedside locker, I asked Jim if he would pull back the curtains and having finished the restocking of the bedside locker, Helen said that she must go and see her manager to update her on the current situation and let her know that she wouldn't be coming in to work for the foreseeable future.

Helen had not long left when Andy arrived at the door of the ward, having made very good time. He paused to register where I was and then walked quickly towards me. Jim helped to me to stand and, making sure not to catch the drip feed, Andy reached in and embraced me. I managed to get my right arm over his shoulder and held him tightly, patting each other's backs in the way that men do. In a cracking voice he said that he had been in touch with Helen on his mobile, while driving up and knew roughly what the situation was. He said, "I don't know what to say" and as we pulled apart, we both had tears welling up in our eyes.

Andy was stood in front of me with Jim just behind him and, in as clear a voice as I could muster, I said to Andy that if what I had been told was true, then things would quickly be out of my hands because I would be on serious pain killing drugs and wouldn't know much about what was going on. Without hesitation he asked what could he do to help? I said that I loved Helen and wanted to be with her as long as I could and I was prepared to undergo some treatment, if it would give me more time with her and Jim, but I told him that the most important thing for me was to die with whatever dignity could be afforded to me and so I asked him solemnly to promise that he would help me to do this. Without a pause for thought he said that he would do whatever he could to uphold my wish.

I looked past Andy's shoulder and saw that Jim was absorbedly evaluating the scene in front of him. Jim looked towards me and as I caught his eyes with mine, I raised my eyebrows and nodded to him to see if he had taken in the meaning behind my words. With tears in his eyes he nodded back, to let me know that he understood.

Helen came to the doorway and when she saw that Andy was there, a look of relief came over her face. She hurriedly made her way down the ward and hugging Andy tightly and kissed him on the cheek. She told him how glad she was to see him, Andy said that he hadn't been there long but that I had managed to give him an update. I could see that Helen had been crying, she said that having just spent the past half hour telling her manager all about it, she was grateful that she would not have to go through the emotional turmoil of explaining it again.

As we stood there I pointed out to Andy the lopsided corner of the bed and with that, he and Jim set about straightening it, I have to say with some gusto, no doubt venting their pent up emotional tensions. After a couple of strong tugs and a few kicks, whatever was holding the corner of the bed down, suddenly released itself and the bed popped up level again. A small victorious outcome which allowed us a brief smile.

It was now close to 8.00pm and it had been a very long and trying day for everyone, which showed in all our faces. I was particularly tired and, as Helen had already arranged for Andy to stay overnight to save him having to drive back South, I said that they should get off home. Following some tearful goodbyes they left the ward, briefly waving back at me before they disappeared along the corridor.

I turned towards the bed and saw my mobile phone on the bedside table, so by carefully manoeuvring the drip stand along with me, I moved around the bed and picked it up.

Using just my right hand I managed to single handedly text to Helen's phone "Missing you already". Within a few moments my phone bleeped and a message appeared on the screen. I clicked on 'Select' and "Missing you too, all my love XXX" flashed onto the small screen.

Having worked my way back round the bed to sit on the newly restored corner and looking towards the ward door with Helen gone from view, the reality that at each parting I would have no way of knowing if we would see each other again really hit home and more tears fell from my bowed head, forming wet patches on the floor where they fell.

Then through my veil of tears, I noticed a blurred white shape approaching me and as I looked up, I could just make out the oval pink form of a face. A hand was placed gently on my shoulder and a woman's voice quietly asked me what the matter was. I could sense genuine compassion in her voice and through the sniffs and the sobs, I managed to wring out the tale of what had gone on and how low I felt. I asked her if she could please pull the curtains around the bed so that I could be on my own. She stood upright and said, "We might be able to do better than that" and with that turned to walk away, my eyes following her diminishing shape as she disappeared out of the ward.

Suddenly I heard someone clapping their hands and at the same time I heard the voice of my lady calling to the other night staff. I couldn't catch what exactly was being said, something about an empty room and I heard my name mentioned as well.

About twenty minutes passed by; I had managed to regain some control by then and had stopped crying. My lady, who I could now see was wearing a white nurse's uniform, accompanied by two other nurses, entered the ward. At her instruction, the other two gathered my belongings from the bedside locker, she then helped me to my feet. As I stood there, somewhat bewildered, she put my gown around my shoulders and then, with her walking besides me pushing the drip stand, the three of us slowly paraded out of the ward and along the corridor in the opposite direction from the one I had come earlier in the day.

Our odd little group processed by the Admissions Ward and then crossed the entrance of another ward; heads turned in both and inquisitive eyes tried to discern what we were up to.

Eventually, we came to a set of fire doors across the corridor. In the wall to my left there was a window and an open door which the nurse in white led us through and we all entered into a small room. I could see that it had a single bed with an ensuite shower and toilet. In the far wall there was a window with the curtains drawn shut and there was an over bed light which had been dimmed. The nurse in white explained that, following the discharge of a patient earlier in the day, the room had now become available and, in her opinion, I was the one in most need of its quiet surroundings and that I should make myself at home.

The two nurses stowed my belongings away once more, while the nurse in white helped me to get onto the bed. She made sure that the drip stand was near to me, and was working properly. Then one of the two nurses piled up the pillows behind me so that I was sat upright and the nurse in white showed me how the bed controls operated and the emergency call button worked. Before she left she asked me if I would like to have an oxygen nose tube.

Thinking that it might help. I accepted, so she went off to locate one and, on her return, she fixed it into the wall socket behind the bed and with a confident, but gentle touch, fitted it to my face. She then drew the curtains to the corridor window and shut the door on her way out. I realised that I hadn't asked the nurse her name and I don't ever remember seeing her again, which made the overall experience very surreal.

Now, for the first time in three days I was on my own, too tired to think, even though my head buzzed with thoughts and images of death and dying and through it all I could envision my lady in white leading me safely to this oasis of quiet calm. My religious education had effectively ended after leaving Sunday school, but I was pretty sure in my mind what angels are supposed to be like, and it seemed to me that she had all the right attributes, even though I was unable tick the box for 'Wings'.

However, even with all this going on, exhaustion took hold and I eventually fell asleep, but it wasn't long before I came crashing awake again, coughing and gasping for air, as though I was drowning. My dodgy larynx had failed me again, but after regaining some composure, I decided to pull a blanket around myself, as best I could, and sit in the chair with my head laid on the side of the bed, and like this I managed to get some sleep.

Wednesday 30th November 2005

I woke fairly early after what must have been a short spell of deep sleep. I had a very stiff neck and shoulder from laying with my upper body prone on the bed. At first, in the half grey light, I wasn't sure where I was but then the awfulness of the previous day came readily to mind. I straightened myself and stood up, determined to give my brain something else to think about and so I set about 'discovering' my new room.

I was interrupted in this task when the 'early' nurse came into the room and the daily functioning of the hospital began in earnest. First, she carried out the ceremony of opening the curtains, which let in the daylight, she then turned her attention to me and proffered a thermometer which she somehow managed to secure under my deformed tongue. Next, she checked my saline drip and when she saw that the bag was empty she removed the line leaving me free from attachments and more able to examine the detail of my surroundings for the first time.

Using the thermometer almost as a pointer, I turned my head about to survey the room. It was basically square and with the curtains opened I was able to see that the window looked out onto a flat roof area, which was surrounded by the high, red brick walls of the other hospital wings, which formed a sort of courtyard area. Although this limited my view, I found that if I lay on the bed I could see the sky and today looked like it was going to be bright and sunny.

The room must have been about 3.5m x 3.5m, and in the centre of the wall facing the foot of the bed there was the door leading into the ensuite toilet and shower room. On the wall opposite the outside window, there was another window which overlooked, and gave borrowed light to, the corridor while the bed head wall had all the hospital paraphernalia you would expect, with pipes, dials and electrical sockets. As well as the wall light, the ceiling had a central recessed florescent fitting and something that I hadn't noticed before - a flat angle poise television with its screen pressed against the wall. To give privacy to the room, each of the windows had a set of curtains whose colour was no doubt supposed to complement the mid-blue of the room.

The high backed chair with wooden arms, which I had slept in the night before, was set between the bed and the outside wall and the bedside locker was on the other side. The usual cantilevered table on wheels, sat at the end of the bed and a small cupboard was positioned under the window to the corridor.

My impression was that, in general, it compared favourably with some of the hotel rooms I had stayed in over the years, and I came to the conclusion that if I had to die somewhere, then this small, warm, private cocoon of a room, would be better than some places I could think of. I took a strange kind of comfort from this thought.

The nurse removed the thermometer and recorded the reading on the bed chart. After she left, I was able to struggle through my ablutions without having to drag the wheeled drip stand around with me and I managed also to avoid knocking the cannula in the back of my left hand which pleased me as it was still quite painful. Once clean and dry, I changed into a clean nightshirt and put on my towelling dressing gown, before sitting in the bedside chair to wait for Helen.

I looked down and saw the blue stitching on the breast pocket of my gown: it read 'HHH'. I smiled, as I remembered that I had bought the robe as a memento of a wonderful weekend that Helen and I had spent at the Hartwell House Hotel in Buckinghamshire and my smile widened, as I was reminded how the 'HHH' had become the family's acronym for 'His Holy Highness' whenever I wore it at home.

There was little to do while I waited, apart from watching the dutiful bed making duo carrying out their task ad nauseum, so time dragged by until Helen arrived. I could have texted her about the new room, but I wanted to see if the change of location could, even for a brief moment, help to lift the hollow eyed expression that had haunted her face the last time I saw her.

My first glimpse of Helen was as she glanced into the room, while passing the corridor window. On entering the room, her initial expression of surprise was soon replaced with a smile, as she took in relative luxury of my new surroundings. She came to where I was sat, leaned forward and kissed me on the forehead. I could see that she was eager to know how it had all come about, so I told her to sit on the bed, while I explained about my mysterious 'lady in white'. I told Helen the way in which the move had been orchestrated, and she said how pleased she was that we would have a measure of privacy over the coming weeks.

Once I had finished my story, Helen told me that she had managed to get hold of our other daughter Kate, who had emigrated to New Zealand with her husband Gary and our two grandchildren Ruby and Ivy. She said that Kate was extremely upset and was making arrangements to fly over to see me as soon as she could. I said that I would be glad to see her.

Helen wanted to know whether, with all the excitement of the move, I had managed to get any sleep, so I told her how I had sat in the chair all night, with my upper body laid across the bed and that this had allowed me to get some fitful dozing between the fits of coughing but I said that after nearly five days of not having a drink, I felt so very thirsty and I was worried that I might lose the ability to swallow altogether. So when the tea trolley came by a short time later, she suggested that maybe I should try to have some milky tea to see if I could swallow it as, after all, I had managed to swallow the jam the previous day.

With a mug of warm tea in my hand, there followed a period of, what can only be described as, extreme tea drinking, with me attempting all sorts of contortions with the cup even to the extent of trying to drink out of the back of it, as you do when you have hiccups, but it was all to no avail: every attempt ended in a coughing fit with tea dripping off my chin and hands and a large stain on my towelling dressing gown and night shirt. Each time, Helen caringly wiped the spilt tea from me, using tissues from the ever present box. I explained to her that the problem was I could not feel where the lukewarm tea was in my mouth and throat, so she suggested that maybe I should try some cold water instead, which I did. However, although I could feel where the water was, it proved every bit as impossible to get down my throat as the lukewarm tea had.

After a few disastrous minutes, Helen agreed that tea drinking had not been one of her best ideas and so we gave up. With her help I changed out of the tea stained dressing gown and night shirt, but so that Helen could take the dirty items home for washing so I had to put on the nightshirt I had worn the day before.

Disaster resolved, I had just got back onto the bed when there was a knock and the door was opened. The consultant came in and said that it was the start of his rounds but before he got side-tracked, he wanted to let me know that he would like to run some more tests, just to see how things were progressing and in the meantime he had arranged for me to have a nasogastric tube inserted, in order that I could be fed using a pump, which he felt would give me sufficient nourishment and all the fluid intake I needed. Having checked whether we had any questions, he then left us on our own again.

We chatted for a while, all the time desperately trying to keep the subject matter as light hearted as possible, both of us acutely aware of the raging undercurrent of each other's emotions. However, as much as we tried to avoid it, we eventually came to the point where the small talk came to an end and we had to deal with the serious matters that lay ahead of us, it was not a conversation that either of us wanted to open.

I took the lead by assuring Helen, as best I could, that I would try to sort things out and hopefully, leave her as little as possible to deal with once I was gone. Helen stopped me at this point by reaching out for my hand. She said that whenever she left the hospital after a visit, her mind was all over the place and so, if she was going to have to make lists of things, she would have to write them down and with that she reached into her voluminous handbag and pulled out a lined note book and a pen.

I told her that my first concern was the business and that I had to see my colleague, Matt, as soon as possible and while I still had lucidity to discuss whether it was his intention to move forward with the company or not. I then said that I needed to see my good friend, Bill. He was due to become the Master of my Masonic Lodge and he had offered me a senior position, working with him for the year starting in December which I would now not be able to fulfil.

Helen was leaning over the pad and I saw a tear fall from her eye onto the page as she formed the words which I could see were forcing her to consider the awful task ahead: that of having to tell so many people about our predicament. There was the extended family, our friends and the people we were linked to through our work and my Masonry. I reached over and took her hand to stop her writing, she looked up and her eyes were brim full, she moved forward in the chair, placed her head on my arm and quietly sobbed.

After a while we managed to carry on, but this only served to press home to me how little time I had left and how my life was petering out, the plans that would not be fulfilled and the people I might never see again. Helen stopped writing and we sat in reflective silence for a few seconds, reluctant to continue, because we knew that the remaining items were going to be the worst of all.

Firstly, I asked Helen if she would make contact with our solicitor, and ask him if he would come into the hospital, so that I could update my will. Secondly I asked if she would get hold of Alan (P), my fiend of nearly fifty years who had, for several years, been in the undertaking business. He had, at my request, as the consequence of a car incident some fifteen years previously, undertaken the responsibility of preparing the body of my son, Justin, and valiantly officiated at his funeral and I hoped that he could find the strength within himself to do the same for me.

With the now lengthy list complete, Helen put the pen and pad back in her handbag, saying that she had no wish to check through it again. She then leaned over so that her head was resting on my chest, just under my chin. I put my good arm across her shoulders and we stayed like this in quiet contemplation until the peace was broken by a knock at the door. Helen lifted her head and said "Come in ", whereupon the door was opened by Gordon.

Gordon ran the clay pigeon shooting club I belonged to, and he also worked for the facilities management company that maintained the hospital. He had just started to ask how I was feeling when a nurse came in, because it was time to do my 'obs'. However, on seeing Gordon and Helen there she offered to come back later if we wanted. Helen looked at me and said she had to put the washing on and make a start on the phone calls and so this would probably be an opportune moment to go home and Gordon, not wishing to delay the nurse, said that he could call back later, so the nurse started to check the various pieces of equipment. As Helen made to leave I asked her if she would be OK. With a shrug she sighed, saying that she thought so, and left as the nurse completed noting the relevant data on the bed chart.

The earlier listing of requests and the inevitability of the outcomes had markedly changed my mood, and sitting in isolation without anything to distract me, I started to envisage how the end might come, how much pain I might be in and, most of all, how I would know when it was over. Unwilling to explore these questions, I puffed up the pillows, laid out on my left side and closed my eyes, hoping that sleep would numb my brain.

I came to sometime later and, through the courtyard window, I could see sunlit white clouds set against the blue sky and, for the briefest of moments, I felt that I must have been having a bad dream but then, as I looked around me at all the hospital paraphernalia, I quickly fell back into the same dark mood I had been in earlier.

There was a knock at the door and Richard, a friend from the village, came into the room. I thanked him for coming but said that I wasn't really up to seeing anyone at the moment. He said he understood but before he left he placed an envelope on the over bed table. When I opened the envelope later, I found that it contained a lovely card with kind, personal comments, and references to an ongoing project in the village, which I had been involved with in my role as Chairman of the Parish Meeting.

Later in the afternoon, two people in white coats entered the room and stood at the foot of the bed, they introduced themselves as trainee doctors. One was shortish, about 5'6" a stocky man of Asian extraction, with a round clean shaven face whose speaking voice made me think that he had probably been born and educated in the UK. The other was taller man, probably 6'0" plus, he was thinner with a thick accent, which made me think that he was probably an overseas student from India or Pakistan, he wore glasses with heavy black rims and he had an exuberant moustache.

They both had pens protruding from the breast pocket of their white coats and each of them wore a stethoscope around their neck, seemingly as a badge of recognition, to mark their status as doctors. However, in all the time they administered to me I never once saw either of them use the instruments.

They confirmed that they had come to fit the nasogastric tube, the moustachioed one proffered a sealed packet for me to see, while the other one laboured under the weight of an open cardboard box containing an electric pump, along with several see through plastic packs of, what I could only describe as looking like, liquidised porridge. They placed all of the kit on the over bed table and asked me if I would move into the chair, which I did.

The taller one of the two seemed to want to take control. Firstly, cleansing his hands with alcohol gel, he opened the pack and took out a thin plastic coiled tube which he proceeded to unroll. Next he moved to the side of the chair and placed one end of the tube in my lap and then by moving his fingers along its length, he started to measure how much of it would be required, first against my stomach, then my chest, followed by my neck and along my cheek, right up to my nose. I can't remember if he marked the tube or whether he just held the position with his thumb and forefinger.

Now the shorter of the two bent down, really close into me and stared up my nostrils, while the other doctor squeezed some lubricant from an applicator onto the end of the tube, then he too also leaned in close and proceeded to insert the tube into my left nostril, and with tiny tentative movements, the tube was very slowly pushed up my nose.

Just then I heard someone come into the room and from the corner of my eye I could see that Helen had arrived, and that she was most amused at the scene being played out in front of her. As I turned my eyes forward again, all I could see was a slowly moving hand with its attendant white sleeve, three wide open eyes, half a pair of glasses and a moustache, the size of a yard broom. All were in very close proximity to me as the progress of the tube became a very intensely observed operation.

All the time the tube was being inserted, I was being asked to keep swallowing and whether the process was at all uncomfortable and to let them know if I needed them to stop, but everything went fine and once a predetermined point on the tube was adjacent to my nose, they both stood upright and smiled, first at me and then at each other. They were obviously very pleased that the tube had been inserted without incident and to hold it in place they secured it to my left cheek using a small sticking plaster. With the tube now inserted they said that the next job was for me to go to the X-Ray Department. I was surprised at this but they explained that it was to have a picture taken of my abdomen, to show them whether the tube was in the correct position or not.

The taller doctor, still the boss it seemed, instructed the shorter one - no 'please' involved - to go and locate a wheelchair. He seemed a little put out by this, no doubt expecting that a porter should have been summoned instead but, realising that this was a forlorn hope, he disappeared out of the door and returned with a wheelchair a short time later. He parked it at the foot of the bed, he then looked at his colleague, then the wheelchair and then at me in quick succession; his puffed out chest and the look on his face, expressing the inner pride he felt for having succeeded in finding one so quickly then, between them, they helped me to transfer from one chair to the other.

Helen said that she would wait until I got back, and with that the pair of doctors set off with some gusto. I don't know what the rush was, but I remember being pushed at breakneck speed down the corridors to the X-Ray Department, receiving several looks of disapproval from those we overtook on the way, and by the time we got to the X-Ray Department they were both panting from their exertions.

Arrangements for the x-ray must have been made before we left the ward, because when we arrived, I was taken straight into a treatment room while the doctors waited outside. The radiographer assisted me out of the chair and asked me to stand in front of a vertical panel. She then moved the x-ray machine into position and disappeared behind a screen. She told me to hold my breath, there was a quick humming noise, followed by a clunk and it was over. The radiographer then came and moved the equipment out of the way and helped me back into the wheelchair. She opened the door to the room and called the two doctors to come in and, while I made myself comfortable for the return journey, the three of them studied my insides on a computer screen. Once satisfied that the tube was correctly sited, the two doctors took me back to my room, luckily at a much more sedate pace than the outward journey.

Back in my room it became obvious that all this was a new experience for the trainee doctors, and it took them several attempts to work out the correct way to connect the electric pump and the food bag to the NG tube and, even when it was connected and secured to the drip stand, they had further difficulties in getting the pump to work at the correct speed. Eventually, the beige coloured mixture slowly started to work its way down the NG tube, and once there was no more visible empty tube to be seen, they stood back to admire their combined efforts and once satisfied, they said their cheerios' and left.

Helen came and stood by the chair and asked me if the NG tube felt uncomfortable, I told her that I couldn't feel it at all really, and she smiled as I recounted the hair-raising journey to the X-Ray Department. I told her that the two doctors, bizarrely, reminded me of Tinga and Tucker, the two little Koala bears from the 60's TV show, the smaller doctor being Tinga and, from then on, these nick names became fixed with us.

Helen had left to collect Jim for evening visiting by the time the consultant called in to see me. He was on his way home and said he wanted to check that the food pump was working correctly and gave the apparatus the once over before nodding his approval. He then said that to help me sleep, he had prescribed a diazepam injection and also some atropine skin patches, the former to help me sleep and the latter to dry up the saliva in my throat and ease my coughing fits. He confirmed that both would be administered by the drugs trolley nurse when she came round in the evening to give me the second of my twice daily penicillin injections.

It must have been around 6.30pm when Helen and Jim got back to the hospital and our daughter Alex, along with her partner Ian, followed shortly behind, having first checked with Helen whether I felt up to seeing visitors. Somehow, Helen had managed to get the nightshirt and towelling robe washed and tumble dried while she was at home, and now laid the folded garments on the cupboard under the corridor window.

By now Jim was getting used to seeing me in hospital but, tonight, the sight of the NG tube up my nose had caught him off guard and all he could think of to ask me was whether I felt anything as the food was pumped through the tube; I assured him that I wasn't in any discomfort. On the other hand, poor Alex looked really pale and drawn. This was the first time she had seen me since she had been told that I had a terminal illness. She came and sat on the chair next to the bed and took hold of my left hand, and in a quiet broken voice, she said that she didn't know what to say, other than she loved me and felt so sad for me and Mum. Helen had hold of my right hand and at this, she gave it a squeeze. I could see, from the redness of her eyes, that Alex had been doing some serious crying before she had come to see me.

We managed to raise the mood and chatted for a bit when Alex, on noticing the angle poise television, asked me whether I had watched any programmes yet. I said that I had not been interested in anything up to now, but that I might want to watch something in the coming days, just to take my mind off things when I was on my own. She perked up at this and said that she had passed the TV card dispensing machine on her way in, so Helen got out her purse and went with Alex to buy a TV card for me.

I was grateful for their visit, but by about 8.30pm I had started to feel exhausted and all I wanted was the diazepam and atropine, to try and get a good night's sleep, so when they returned with the TV card, I told Helen and the others that I was very tired. They said that they understood and so would make a move but, before she left, Helen collected together a bag of dirty laundry, which hereafter would become a regular chore. Once they had said their goodbyes I just lay on the bed, waiting for the drugs trolley, too tired even to watch the television.

Soon after they had gone the drugs trolley nurse arrived with two packs of the NG food balanced on the top. She set about giving me the penicillin and diazepam injections, both of them through the valve in the cannula on the back of my hand, and then, having stuck the atropine patch on my upper left arm, she asked me if I wanted to settle down for the night. I nodded that I would, so using the controller, she inclined the top end of the bed and set up my pillows. Once I was comfortable she connected one of the food packs to the pump. Tinga and Tucker had told me that this would run all night, to give me most of the food while I was sleeping and therefore give me more freedom to move about during the day. The nurse made sure that the pump was working properly and then left.

Apart from some fitful dozing, I had been pretty much awake continuously for over 60 hours and I desperately needed to sleep. I tried lying in different positions, to see if I could manage to be on my back without triggering a coughing fit, and after a few attempts I found that if I lay diagonally across the bed, from right foot end to left head end, and tilted my head to the left, there was less irritation. So having settled into this position, I used the controller to dim the over bed light, and with the help of the atropine patches I finally fell into a deep sleep, the first in nearly four days.

Well into the night, the effect of the atropine caused me to come to with a horribly dry throat, my tongue felt swollen and stuck to the roof of my mouth and I was desperate for some water, so that I could at least try to wet the inside of my mouth.

I got out of bed and started to walk towards the shower room, but I had completely forgotten about the NG tube, or my being attached to the food pump and as the tube and electric cable extended to their fullest extent, I suddenly felt the sticking plaster being plucked from my cheek. Before I could react, the whole of the NG tube exited my nose in one continuous motion and fell to the floor. In the dim light I was stunned to see the whole tube lying snake like at my feet, with the food continuing to exude from its 'mouth', while the pump continued to whirr away. As I stood transfixed in my nightgown, watching the chaos, I tried to coax my brain into some kind of lucidity to make sense of these surreal events.

After a few moments, it came to me out of the mist of confusion that I must turn off the pump, so reaching behind the bedhead I found the socket and flicked the switch, then, trying not to step in the puddle of goo on the floor, I slowly moved around the bed so that I could press the emergency button. In the quiet of the night they work really well and it was only a matter of seconds before I heard hurried footsteps in the corridor and the door was opened by a worried looking nurse. On seeing me out of bed, she asked what the problem was. All I could do was stare at the floor and point to the still expanding sea of refined porridge, so she switched on the main light to see what I was pointing at.

The nurse quickly assessed the situation and told me to wait there while she went to get something to clean it up. She must have also called for assistance because, just after she returned with some paper towels to clean the floor, Tinga arrived, looking very sleepy indeed. He asked me had I hurt myself and I told him not as far as I knew.

Tinga sat me in the chair and said that he would have to insert another NG tube and left to go and collect one from the store. He was gone for what seemed like ages, so long in fact that the nurse had time to clean the floor, wipe it over with a damp cloth, and remove the now virtually empty food pack from the drip stand and clear it away, during which time I had finally managed to use the loo.

When Tinga got back he apologised for taking so long, he explained that when he got to the store there were no adult NG tubes so he had made a detour to the Children's Ward and managed to get a child's one, which he thought should be alright until the morning when it could be changed again for an adult one.

He sat me in the chair and repeated the process he and Tucker had used earlier in the day, but over the intervening period it seemed that he must have become something of an expert, or possibly that he was already much better at it than Tucker, because he quickly managed to insert the new NG tube while just asking me to swallow as he did it. I asked him if, this time, he could use a bigger plaster to hold the NG tube, so he found some kind of wound dressing, about 3" square, and said, "There, that should do it". I thought that next I would be trundled back to the X-Ray Department as before, but no, not this time. He just asked me to get back into bed, fitted a new food pack to the pump and, having checked that everything was working as it should, he said that he hoped that I would be able to sleep and then left, followed by the nurse, who switched the light off as she closed the door.

It's difficult trying to get back to sleep when something like this has happened and so I lay there, awake in the near darkness, for at least a couple of hours, but in those waking moments I did some serious thinking about what I needed to do while I was still capable, and I knew that however unpleasant a prospect, I would need to find a way to talk to Helen about these difficult subjects when she came in later and with that settled in my mind I must have dozed off.

Thursday 1st December 2005

I was woken by the noise of the early nurse coming into the room. She noticed that the pump had completely emptied the food packet, so she switched off the pump and disconnected the tube. I always got a great sense of freedom when the nurses did this because it meant I could move about without having to wheel the drip stand with me.

The nurse asked me how I was feeling this morning. With my broken voice I tried to explain to her, as best I could, all about the shenanigans of the night before. She cocked her eyebrow in surprise at the story, and asked me whether I had managed to get any sleep with all that going on. I said that it had kept me awake for long periods, but overall, I had managed to sleep for about three hours and I was feeling a bit brighter. She smiled and seemed genuinely pleased for me. She asked me if I wanted to have the next food bag fitted straight away or wait until after I had used the bathroom. I said would she mind leaving it for the time being and so she left to continue her duties elsewhere.

The small oblong mirror in the shower room was fitted quite high on the wall over the hand basin, so all I could really see was my head and shoulders. The reflected image this morning was not at all an attractive sight. My lack of shaving meant that I had started to grow a beard and it was the first time that I had really seen the NG tube. Although now disconnected, it was still full of the beige food stuff, looking all the world like a droopy piece of spaghetti hanging from my nose (*I was starting to have these surreal imaginings*) and my hair was standing on end like a cock's-comb. The whole impression was the nearest I had seen myself to looking like a punk rocker, with the NG tube reminding me of a body piercing.

I thought that I had better tidy myself up a bit before everyone came in. Try as I might, I couldn't take off my tee shirt so, with it still in place, I used my one good arm to wet down my hair. This immediately changed my reflected image from 'Johnny Rotten' to the keyboard player in 'Sparks'. Then, trying desperately not to get my tee shirt wet, I managed to lather and shave my face, carefully manoeuvring the razor around the sticking plaster and NG tube. I reviewed my amended appearance in the mirror, and felt that I had not done a bad job, considering I had only been able to use one arm.

The next task was to put on my gown. I hung the collar on the coat peg and pushed my right arm down the sleeve and then, using the same arm, I felt around the collar and, having lifted it off the coat peg, I pulled the rest of the gown over my left shoulder. Panting at the exertion, I sat in the chair to wait for Helen to arrive. While I waited, the same bed linen duo from the day before, came in and performed a fascinating and efficient sheet change. I found that I was starting to watch even mundane tasks, like changing bed linen, with an all absorbing intensity, just to help time pass by.

It was not long after when Helen entered the room, her smile was a real sight for sore eyes. She has always been a smart, elegant woman and now the tear stained cheeks and untended hair of the previous couple of days were gone, she had made sure that she looked her very best for me. Coming across to the chair she gave me a big hug, and kissed me on the shaved cheek and realising that it was now smooth, she stood back and admired my efforts at sartorial splendour. I have to give her credit for holding her smile and not laughing out loud.

My voice was still no more than a husky whisper, but I managed to repeat to Helen the story I had told the nurse earlier. She was concerned initially, but as no harm had been done, she could also see the funny side and was also pleased that I had finally managed to get some decent sleep. She asked me how I was getting on with the NG tube, now that it was back in place, I said that I knew that I was supposed to be getting all of my sustenance from the NG porridge, but whether it was the atropine patches or because I couldn't drink any fluids, I had a raging thirst.

Changing the subject, Helen said that she had managed to make some phone calls and that Bill had said that he would come to see me that afternoon. Unfortunately though, our solicitor was on holiday until the following Wednesday. She said that his secretary had asked whether I wanted to see anyone else, but I told Helen that I would rather wait until he got back than discuss our private matters with someone we didn't know.

The consultant knocked on the door and came into the room; it was the start of his rounds. He explained to us that because the tumour would eventually have a significant effect on my brain and nervous system, it had been decided that my case was to be taken over by a specialist neurological consultant. This chap split his time between Hereford and Birmingham hospitals and, as today was one of his visit days, he would call in to see me when he had finished his morning clinics. However, the consultant said that out of interest he would continue keeping an overall watching brief, because mine was an unusual medical condition.

It was about midday when, as expected, the neurological consultant came in. I was sitting in the chair with Helen sat on the bed holding my hand. He smiled and introduced himself and went on to explain in more detail how he thought my condition had arisen and in what way the symptoms of the growing cancer might develop. He said that, over time, the paralysis would become more extensive, which would eventually lead to a final closing down of my lung and heart function. He then leaned closer and his voice became quieter. He said that he was sorry that he couldn't offer actual timings on this, because it would all depend on how aggressive the cancer turned out to be but, unfortunately, he felt that the overall life expectancy we had been given was probably about right.

At this news, Helen's grip tightened, she could no longer maintain her stoicism, her shoulders heaved and floods of tears came, all I could do was reach across with my right arm and pull her head onto my shoulder and try to comfort her, I think that the consultant was also affected by Helen's outpouring because he stood upright again and turned his head away.

After a while, Helen was able to regain some composure, she reached for some tissues to dab at her eyes and wipe her nose, and then she apologised to the consultant who seemed almost embarrassed. He replied saying that she had absolutely no need to apologise and that he just wished that he could give us better news. Helen and I just sat looking at each other gripping each other's hands tightly, there were things that needed to be said but, we instinctively knew that this was not the time.

The consultant was at pains to say that as far as he could tell, from the fact that my paralysis seemed to have plateaued slightly that the tumour was not growing aggressively at the moment. However, he would like to try and determine more accurately the extent and actual makeup of the tumour. To this end he wanted me to have an MIR scan but, having already checked the lists he had found, because it was close to the weekend, that they were all full so he had arranged for me to have a scan on Monday morning, still in time for the results to be available for his next visit. He also said that he wanted to test the fluid in my spinal column for cancer cells and so he had also arranged for me to have a lumber puncture which would be carried out later that day. He asked if we had any questions before he left. I think that we were still too stunned at this final confirmation to think of anything.

After he had gone, Helen and I tried to look on the positive side and we both felt that if the consultant was still looking for more details then, just possibly, he might come up with a different outcome, so our mood lifted a little. Looking to change the subject, which was fast becoming her forte, Helen asked me whether I had tried the over bed TV yet, and when I said no, she set about persuading me to have a go. So we spent a distracted 15-20 minutes working out where the card slot was, how to plug in the earphones and which buttons to press on the controller.

It was the first time I had used a flat screen TV and I must say that I was impressed with the quality of the picture. We had just got it all working when there was a knock at the door and Bill walked in. Pleased to see him, I switched off the TV and removed the headphones. Helen, seeing that Bill and I needed to talk, said she could do with a cup of tea and asked him if he would like her to fetch a cup for him, Bill accepted her offer and as Helen left the room he came and sat in the chair next to the bed.

Bill was in his late seventies and I knew him to be a very caring person. He reached over and took my hand and said that he was very fond of both me and Helen and that he had been terribly upset on receiving her phone call about our desperate situation. With tears in his eyes and a quavering voice, he told me that he had contacted a good number of the Lodge Brethren who, although not wanting to disturb us, had all asked him to say that they were thinking of and praying for us both at this sad time, and some had also sent more personal messages which Bill repeated.

When Helen returned she found both Bill and I upset from our having discussed what might have been. As Helen handed him the cup of vending machine tea, Bill cleared his throat and thanked her and, after he had taken a couple of sips, was more his old self again. The three of us then spent a while, reminiscing about the times we had spent together, particularly one time on the golf course. It had been a warm sunny afternoon and Helen had come for a walk with us as Bill and I hacked our way round eighteen holes. We all agreed that we had seen much happier times. Eventually though, the conversation ran dry and Bill said that he needed to go, because he still had a lot of preparation for his big night which was a week the following Monday. With that we thanked him for coming and he wished us an emotional farewell. It had been a very upsetting time for all of us and from his demeanour, I didn't think that he was contemplating making another visit and for the first time Helen and I came to the realisation that there would be many people beyond our own close family and friends who would be affected by my demise.

The rest of the afternoon passed with the hospital operating around us in its usual, almost automated, fashion. Nurses moved to and fro, attending to patients and creating the background hubbub of busy people and, as much as we tried to put it off, the time came when Helen had to make the move home for Jim.

It was a particularly hard time for him at the moment; he was in the final stages of his 'A' level education and was having to deal with all the stressful emotions of having a terminally ill father when, what he should have been doing, was preparing for the Spring exams. Helen and I were both worried that the chances of him being able to concentrate, with everything that was going on, were pretty slim and so we had agreed early on, that it was important for her to try and keep his regime as normal as possible; we felt that it was all we could do to give him a fighting chance.

While she was away I busied myself with the over bed TV and became absorbed with a history programme on UKTV, which is not a channel we had at home.

Early evening saw Helen and Jim back at the hospital. I recounted to Jim what the new consultant had said about further tests and a little later, as if almost on cue, Tinga and Tucker appeared at the door. They asked if it would be OK to prep me for the lumber puncture which they were intending to carry out after visiting hours, so Helen and Jim said that they would step out into the corridor for a moment while they did it. I think that they saw it as an opportunity to have a break and restore their emotions.

The doctors asked me to roll on my right side and Tucker explained that they he was going to give me several anaesthetic injections to the area of my back where they needed to be insert the epidural needle into my backbone. He said that once done they would leave me for a while for the anaesthetic to take effect and would then return after visiting time to carry out the lumber puncture and with that he asked me to adopt the foetal position. Tinga adjusted my clothing and wiped my exposed back with an alcohol swab before Tucker proceeded with the injections.

I'm not sure how many they had decided were necessary, but after the first couple of scratches I didn't feel much at all, because the anaesthetic was starting to work. When it was all done Tinga rubbed my skin again with the swab and they left saying that they would be back later.

Time passed. Helen and Jim had, by now, returned to the room and finished their drinks and, as the end of visiting time approached, we started to wonder where the doctors had got to. More time went by and eventually they returned, apologising for the delay and saying that they had been called to deal with an emergency.

They asked me to roll on my side again and tested the area of my back with the cap of a pen. Tucker asked me if I could still feel anything, to which I gave an affirmative answer. Somewhat surprised at this, Tucker, who again seemed to be taking charge, asked Tinga if he would go and get another dose of anaesthetic. Helen realising that it was starting to get late and that this could take some time said that she thought now would be a good time for her and Jim to leave and so we said our goodbyes.

I had been a bit apprehensive ever since the consultant had said he wanted me to have an epidural, because 25 years previously I had needed to have it done a couple of times as treatment for an injured back and it had not been a pleasant experience, so this delay was starting to vex me somewhat.

When Tinga got back with the additional anaesthetic, Tucker injected it into my back in three or four places, then they both left again, but this time they returned in about twenty minutes and having tested the numbness of the area again, and finding it satisfactory, Tucker decided that he was going to proceed with the lumber puncture.

He asked me to get into the foetal position once more and to try to hold onto to my legs, because it was important that I should stay steady while he inserted the needle into my spine, so I curled up on the bed and tried to cradle my knees, as tightly as I could, with my good arm. From this position I could not see what Tucker was doing, but I felt a pressing sensation on my back as though he was feeling where he needed the needle to go in and then I felt the pressure point release as the needle broke the skin, but there was no pain. I heard Tinga and Tucker mumbling to each other but I could not make out what they were saying.

The next sensation I felt was as if the end of the needle was grating on the surface of my backbone, this went on for a bit as though Tucker was trying to find the gap between my vertebrae; then he said could I please curl up more tightly. I tried to but it was to no avail, because he still seemed unable to find the gap he was searching for. Having failed he said that he was sorry, but that he would have to try again in another position. I thought, "Great, not only am I going to die soon, but at this rate I may well end up disabled to boot!"

He went through the whole process once more, but again all I could feel was the grating sensation, seemingly on the surface of the bone but thankfully still without pain. All the time this was going on, Tinga and Tucker's mumblings were becoming louder and more agitated, but still at a level where my less than acute hearing could discern their meaning. Then, with a frustrated sigh, Tucker removed the needle from my back and I heard the syringe clang into the metal dish. He said that he was having some difficulty and needed to go and discuss the matter with a colleague and that he would be back shortly.

With that he left the room instructing Tinga to stay and keep an eye on things. I stayed as tightly curled up as I could manage because I was worried that if I moved I might cause myself further injury. I jokingly said to Tinga that I supposed his mate had gone for the instruction manual, but the attempt at humour fell on deaf ears.

Maybe twenty minutes or so passed during which time Tinga, who seemed to be getting anxious at the length of the wait, went to the door on a couple of occasions to see if Tucker was coming back. I think maybe he was worried that he had done a runner and left him with the problem. However, Tucker eventually reappeared at the door, this time closely followed by a Chinese gentleman. In a quiet voice, he asked the other two what my name was to which he received a mumbled answer. He said "Good evening Mr Wilding", and told me his name, he then said that Doctor

[*Tucker*] had asked him to assist with this procedure and could I please curl up really tightly and stay very still. With that the new doctor took the syringe and with no problem at all felt along my spine, inserted the needle into the spinal cavity, removed the required amount of fluid and replaced the syringe back in the metal dish all within a minute I should guess. He said "All done Mr Wilding" and then I heard him tell Tinga and Tucker, in a low angry voice, that he had helped them out this time, but if ever either of them called him out again he would report them, and with that he left at some pace.

Tinga and Tucker finished up by wiping my back with a swab and applying a dressing and said that I should lay as I was for a few minutes before carefully rolling onto my back and that I would be alright to move freely in about an hour's time.

I found out later that Tucker had been unable to find the right place to insert the needle and so he had gone to the maternity department and summoned the assistance of the anaesthetist, because he was experienced at giving epidural pain relief injections to pregnant women. I suppose I should thank Tucker for not stumbling on with the procedure himself and possibly causing me an injury. It can't have been easy for him to go to another department and admit that he was unable to complete the lumber puncture.

By now, what with all the goings-on, I was emotionally exhausted and completely knackered and I fell asleep, on top of the bed, still in the foetal position, which is how the nurse found me when she came with the drugs trolley. She had to wake me up and help me into my nightshirt, before she could administer my sleeping draft and apply the atropine patch. She then settled me into bed and connected the NG tube to a new food packet and I fell asleep to the soft whirring of the electric pump.

I did wake in the night to rinse my dry mouth out with cold water, but I managed to avoid a repeat of the previous night's palaver.

Friday 2nd December 2005

I came to when the early nurse breezed into the room and opened the curtains. I found that I couldn't even manage to mumble "Morning!" to her, because my tongue was seemingly super glued to the roof of my mouth. Obviously the atropine patches had excelled themselves and, in the hope of getting some flexibility back into it, the only thing I could think to do was swill my mouth out with cold water. So, having carefully unplugged my food pump from the electrical socket, I wheeled the drip stand into the shower room where, firstly, I nodded to my reflection in the mirror, probably more than anything, just to acknowledge the fact that I was still alive and then I bent over the wash basin and set to, rather ungainly, trying to slurp water from the running cold tap.

Having partially succeeded in my goal, I returned to sit in the chair, where I could now see the world, well the sky anyway, out of the window. Realising how dehydrated I must have been for my tongue to have done this, I started to get concerned that I wasn't getting enough fluids and, although I had past the SALT test earlier in the week, albeit with some difficulty, I was none the less anxious that if I didn't swallow some liquid soon I might lose the ability altogether; but so far all attempts at trying different liquids had ended in messy ignominy.

With my mouth still feeling like a drought cracked field, I noticed that the water jug still had some small, un-melted, pieces of ice cube in it. I wondered what would happen, if I put a small piece of the ice in my mouth and let it melt, it might be that my damaged throat could cope with such a small amount of liquid.

Having decided, "Nothing ventured nothing gained", I fiddled around in the jug of water with my fingers, trying to grab some of the slippery ice and having finally managed to pinch a piece between my thumb and forefinger I carefully placed it into my mouth.

Initially the ice melted slowly and a fine trickle of cool liquid passed into my throat but then, as the ice melted more quickly, the extra liquid got past my damaged larynx and into my airway, causing a convulsive coughing fit.

Now, on previous occasions, these attempts at swallowing had ended up with the uncontrolled ejection of the contents of my mouth, i.e. messy ignominy but, on this occasion, while inhaling after the first bout of coughing, the remaining piece of ice slid down my throat, (*If it had it gone the same way as the water goodness knows what might have happened*) and afterwards, as I drew breath, I realised that I had felt the small piece of ice go down my throat, I had actually felt the swallow; it was like someone had switched a light on in my brain.

I was eager to see whether I could actually repeat this on purpose, rather than by accident, so I fished around in the jug for another piece of ice and once again placed it in my mouth. Trying to be a bit more methodical this time, I cocked my head over my left shoulder and worked the ice along the inside of my cheek, until I could feel it on my tongue at the back of my mouth, then with one movement, I tried to squeeze my tongue against the roof of my mouth while, at the same time, carrying out an exaggerated action, similar to that of a tortoise reaching for a proffered lettuce leaf. Bingo! I could feel the ice go all the way down and, apart from a slight involuntary chest heave, the whole process had been a success.

It was the type of happenstance that gives you an unexpected uplift, a little glimmer of hope which enables you to push back, against what had become the ever present weight of an inevitable outcome, my only disappointment was that there was no-one there with whom to share my achievement.

Emboldened by my success I had another go, and another, until the last couple of pieces of ice had gone, but still wanting to practice my new skill, I knew that I had to find a way to secure a new supply. A cunning plan came to mind. Firstly, taking the jug in hand I shuffled my way to the shower room and poured most of the water into the sink, I then returned to the room where I sat in the chair and pushed the call button. It wasn't long before I heard hurried footsteps, as the nurse came down the corridor.

When she appeared at the door, I managed to get across to her that I would like some more iced water, whereupon she gave me a very old fashioned look, as much as to say, "The call button is for crises only and NOT for summoning room service". However, with all good grace she took the jug away and returned a short time later with another which, I was pleased to see, had a full complement of ice cubes that clinked together as she placed the jug on the table.

Eager to practice this new, secret skill, I waited until the nurse had left the room. I then moved the jug from the table and placed it on the seat of the chair, making sure it was held fast between my knees. Then using my good arm, I reached into the jug and took an ice cube from the water, at which point I was immediately struck by a major oversight in my planning, the new supply of ice had not had any time to melt, they were all full size ice cubes and there was no way I was going to be able to swallow one of them whole.

I tried to nibble off a corner of the ice cube with my front teeth, but I could only manage to scrape off a few shavings, which quickly turned to water in my mouth. Cue a coughing fit and lap full of cold water as the jug wobbled and the water slopped out. I dropped the ice cube back into the jug and once again shuffled my way to the shower room, where I managed to squeeze most of the wet out of my nightshirt using the hand towel.

Unable to avoid sitting on the cold wet fabric of my pyjama trousers, I carefully lowered myself back onto the chair. I then took another ice cube from the jug, but this time, before proceeding, I placed the jug back on the table so as not to have to suffer the consequences of any more spillages.

I looked around the room, but couldn't see anything that I could use to break up the ice cube, so there was no alternative but to put the whole thing in my mouth and break it up using my back teeth.

I knew that this could be fraught with all sorts of problems, but I couldn't see an alternative, so carefully placing the ice cube in my mouth and turning my head over my left shoulder I bit down, quick and hard, not wanting to extend contact between my teeth and the ice for any longer than necessary. The result was that the ice cube exploded, so I quickly leaned forward to let the broken ice fall into my open left hand, which was resting in my lap. I sorted through the debris and picking up one of the larger pieces with my right hand then went through my ice swallowing trick once more. Satisfied with my achievement I sat back in the chair inwardly, and probably outwardly, smiling at my success.

I could hardly contain my excitement and must have still had a Cheshire Cat smile right across my face when Helen arrived. Her face took on a quizzical expression when she could see that I looked much happier than of late, and no sooner had she taken off her coat and sat on the bed, than I began to whisper breathlessly to her about the new swallowing trick that I had learnt using the ice cubes. She said that she was very happy for me and insisted that I show her straight away, so I fished around in the jug and managed to find one of the, by now, smaller pieces of ice floating in the water and proceeded to demonstrate my new found skill. Once I had successfully gone through the whole process, Helen put her arms around my shoulders and kissed my forehead.

The rest of the morning followed its usual pattern of events and after the nurse replaced the food bag I asked Helen if she thought it would be OK for us to go for a walk, just to get my legs moving a bit. She thought it was a good idea and suggested that we could try and walk as far as the Nurses' Station and back to see how I got on.

Helen helped me to put on my gown, and then I reached across the back of the chair and unplugged the food pump from the wall socket. The pump unit had a battery backup system so that it could work independently of the electrical supply so, finally being fully mobile, Helen opened the door and for the first time since I had arrived in the room, I ventured tentatively into the corridor.

After the first few steps I started feeling a bit light headed, but we decided to continue, and after a slow shuffle we achieved our goal of reaching the Nurses' Station. Helen said that I shouldn't do too much on the first occasion, so we turned around and headed back to the room. On the way we passed one of my regular nurses who smiled and said she was pleased to see me out and about.

When we got back to the room Helen helped me get back onto the bed, and made sure that the food pump was properly plugged back into the mains. Seeing me flaked out, she said that it was probably a good time for her to get off home so that I could have a rest in time for visiting, she said that she expected other family members would have arrived by then and be wanting to see me.

After she had left and, as I didn't have the attraction of the meal trolley to look forward to for, I plugged the card into the TV in and switched through a few channels. I found that I didn't have any interest in the news programmes. I think mainly because it seemed pretty pointless to me to learn about things that might not be resolved in my remaining short lifetime, so I chose one of the history programmes instead. I plugged in the ear phones and tried to watch a programme about what the Romans had done for us, but I couldn't really take it in because of my anxious anticipation of what might happen later.

I don't want to sound ungrateful in any way, but I feared that the evening's visiting time would be a very testing time for everyone. Of course Helen and Jim would be coming and my brother Andy would be returning, bringing his wife Sue with him and I had been told by Helen that my sister Diane and her daughter Katherine would be coming as well but, however dire my situation seemed, I had at least been involved with the dread of it for some time, which had slightly taken the edge off of the awfulness of it; but this would be the first time, particularly the latter three, had seen me since they had been told of my impending death. It also meant that this would be the first opportunity for them to release their emotions to me about it, and I knew that I would have to respond in equal measure to each of them.

They started arriving about 7.00pm, Helen and Jim first, then the others, each one tentatively entering the room in solemn mood, not sure what they would see or how bad I would look. I tried to put on a welcoming face with as much of a smile as I could muster, but it proved very upsetting as one by one they came to the bedside and said how sad they were to find me in such a parlous state. Gradually, as we all talked and reminisced, things seemed to get beyond the initial tearful stage, but then, after about half an hour, some other friends arrived from the South Coast, plunging the whole gathering into sombre mood once more.

I was finding the emotional energy of it all very draining and, after a while, Helen, seeing that I was starting to fade, suggested to everyone that as they were all staying at the house over the weekend, it might be better to let me rest now so that I would be refreshed for the next day's visiting. They all readily agreed and after some tearful farewells they left, leaving Helen and me to say good night.

Until now I had craved the visits of Helen and Jim, because they brought a certain amount of normality to what was otherwise a very abnormal situation but now being on my own brought a real sense of relief. However, in the quiet if my room I realised that this was how things would be for the next two days.

Andy had told me that many others of my family and friends were coming to visit and I could see that it would be my responsibility to receive their emotional farewells with gentleness and humility. The thought of saying goodbye to so many people seemed to bring home to me the finality of my situation and, on top of the emotion of the earlier visits, I was unable to hold back the tears.

After a while there was a quiet knock at the door and the new consultant opened the door. He came across to the bed and said that, although it was late, he thought that he would call in on his way home from Birmingham to let me know as soon as possible that the test on my spinal fluid had shown it was clear of cancer cells. I thanked him, but after he left, and in a state of hopeless frustration at the news, I picked up the phone and texted to Helen "They keep telling me that I am going to die, but all the tests come back negative!" She must have had the phone at her side, because she texted me back almost straight away saying that at least it was some good news at last. She ended the text by saying that she loved me and would see me in the morning.

There was another knock at the door and the drugs trolley nurse came in and gave me my penicillin injection and fitted the atropine patch. I reached up to turn out the over bed light and tried to settle down to sleep.

Weekend - Saturday 3rd and Sunday 4th December

I had actually had a reasonable night's sleep and only woke when the 'early' nurse came into the room, and when she opened the curtains I could see that the weather was set to be fair. I looked at my phone to see if anyone had texted me and saw the date. I realised that it was my Dad's birthday, and I remembered that the last time I had seen him alive was in 1974, lying unconscious in a hospital bed in Winchester. I raised an imaginary glass in a toast to his memory and said to myself, "Happy Birthday Dad, see you soon".

Hospitals become strange places at the weekend, the routines and faces change, there is far less hustle and bustle and the people you have come to trust to stick needles in you each day have gone. The few nurses who are left do their best, but first need to know what has happened to you so, as each one arrives at your bedside, looks at the notes and then asks about your condition. If, like me, you have very little voice, you wish they would give you a placard with the details on it to hang around round your neck, so that you don't have to repeat the story time and again.

The only text I had received was the one that Helen had sent the previous evening, so knowing that folk would be arriving from about 10.00am onwards I decided that I had better get going. The food bag was not empty, but I switched the pump off and disconnected the NG tube anyway and headed to the shower.

I made a special effort to wash and shave this morning and with my one good arm even managed to rinse through my hair, however, cleaning my teeth with a brush proved to be a complete 'No no', and so using my finger, I rubbed toothpaste around the inside of my cheeks and, by leaning forward over the basin, I was able to rinse the residue away. I even managed to dig out the deodorant spray from my wash bag and give my underarms a squirt, after all there was going to be a lot of close proximity today and being smelly wasn't the last memory I wanted people to have of me.

I put on a pair of track suit bottoms and struggled into a polo shirt so that I would look reasonable for people when they arrived. I moved the chair as close to the back wall as I could, without interfering with the feed pump, and then sat down, I then reconnected my NG tube to the pump and switched it back on. However, realising that there was still quite some time to wait, and feeling apprehensive about how the day would turn out, I got up and moved the TV to where I could see it from the chair, plugged in the earphones and sat down to watch another documentary, in an effort take my mind off of things and settle my nerves.

Helen and Alex arrived a bit earlier than usual. I think as much as anything, Helen wanted to make sure that I was presentable, so she was pleasantly surprised to set me ready to receive visitors. Andy arrived about twenty minutes later along with nephews and nieces and other family members who proceeded to take up residence in the Visitors' Lounge. Andy, as acting subaltern, then marshalled them into small groups to come and visit me, and after a while one group would leave to be replaced by another and so it continued.

In the first round of visits, some would arrive in tears, while the faces of others showed the disbelief they found themselves in, trying to rationalise the situation. Because of my damaged throat and lack of voice, much of the conversation tended to be stilted, with little exchanged beyond utterances of sympathy, and how on earth this could be happening to me but, as the day wore on and people were on their second or third visit, the topic of conversation became lighter and, by late afternoon, we were managing to reminisce about the past and the good times we had spent in each other's company. So, although it had been stressful at the beginning of the visits, as time went on we could find little things to smile about, and the mood was a more relaxed.

Helen, for the most part, stayed to comfort and bolster me but, from time to time, the emotion of it all would get to her and she would have to leave to regain her own composure before returning to my side.

Sometime early in the afternoon Matt arrived, having driven straight to the hospital from Southampton. We talked briefly of what would happen to the company after I had gone but it was not a subject that either of us wanted to dwell on. However, in order for him to be able to keep things on an even keel in the meantime, he asked me if I would give him the access codes to my computer, so that he could see what appointments he may have to cancel, invoices to send, or money to chase etc. So with Andy's help I made a list and, after assuring me that whatever happened he would make sure that Helen would be looked after by the company, Matt left to go to the house and sort out what he could.

By about 6.00pm I was starting to feel very tired and my irritating coughing fits were becoming more frequent. It was now dark outside and some of the visitors had already made their way back to the house, so that they could start preparing food for those who were going to stay overnight. Seeing how tired I was becoming, Helen suggested to Andy that, as it had been a long day for everyone, particularly me, it would be best if I had some peace and quiet so that I could be ready for visiting again the next day.

After all the goodbyes and hand waves, as people left the room, I received a final hug and a kiss from Helen, followed by a quick wave as she passed the corridor window and then I was on my own again. My head was still swimming with the thoughts and sounds of the day, remembering all the people who had been there and snippets of the things that had been discussed. I tried to clear my head, but couldn't, so I lay down on the bed and swung the TV around to where I could see it. I clicked through the channels until I found another history programme, and just steeped my overactive brain cells in the narration to try and calm things down.

Half an hour or so went by and, realising that I wasn't following the programme at all, I flicked the 'Off' switch on the TV controller, and removed my earphones before laying back onto the pillows. As I rested there, it surfaced in my consciousness, that there were those who had visited today, some of whom I had known for the greater part of my life, whose visit tomorrow would probably be the last time that we would set eyes on each other. I started to feel very sad indeed.

I was still in this reflective mood when the drugs trolley nurse came in; it was time to start the night time NG food and have the penicillin injection and atropine patch. In order for the tubes and wires to be connected, the nurse helped me put on a nightshirt so that I could get into bed. Having sorted out all the technical stuff, she informed me that they had run out of atropine patches and wouldn't be able to get any more until Monday. This was very troubling because it was only the drying effect of the patches that was keeping my throat clear of mucus, which allowed me to get any reasonable sleep. The nurse was very apologetic, but said unfortunately there was nothing she could do and hoped that I would not be too badly affected during the night. She then noted what she had done on the bed chart and left.

Frustrated at this news, and with no-one else to talk to, I looked around for my phone and texted this latest information to Helen. She texted back, saying that she would try and sort something out in the morning during visiting, and added all her love with a line of XXXXXs.

Resigned to having a disturbed night, I piled up the pillows so as to keep my head nearly upright and in this way the first part of the night didn't go too badly, but as time went by the niggling cough started again and became a real problem.

I struggled on like this for a bit, but later, after I returned from using the loo, having been very careful not to repeat the electrical flex limitation issues, I decided not to get back into the bed, but rather set the chair adjacent to it instead. In this way I hoped that I might be able to sleep, head forward on the bed, as I had done before and, with the food pump's gentle whirring noise providing a soothing lullaby, I managed to get some relief from the overwhelming tiredness of the long emotional day.

In the morning, the 'early' nurse gently woke me and said that she was surprised to find me out of bed, asleep in the chair. She disconnected the empty food bag and opened the curtains, and then asked me if I needed any help to get ready for the day ahead. I thanked her but said I felt that I could manage. Before leaving the room she turned and said that she liked my family and friends. I must have raised my eyebrows in a quizzical expression, so she explained that the previous day, they had pretty much taken over the Visitors' Room for the whole day, where they had spent their time chatting, reading or doing puzzles and that they had quietly come and gone so that they did not disturb other patients, which was not always the case with other visitors. I thanked her and said that it was nice of her to mention it; she smiled an acknowledgement and left.

Having sorted out my ablutions I got dressed. A nurse came in and took my 'obs', recording the data on the bed chart and then I sat in the chair and waited. Helen and Jim arrived first, followed by Andy and the others, there were also some new faces. Andy shepherded in the first group of visitors, so Helen said that it was a good time for her to go and see the nurse about the atropine patches and with that, disappeared back into the corridor.

It was quite a while before she returned, with a look of disappointment on her face. She said that, having approached someone at the Nurses' Station, they had gone off to search for some patches, but could only manage to confirm that there were none available and that it would have to be sorted on Monday, which was not the news I had hoped for.

About lunch time, Alan (P) and his wife Sue arrived. I asked Andy if Helen and I could have some time alone with them to discuss the funeral arrangements. Once Andy had stemmed the flow of visitors and the room had cleared, I asked Alan to come close. I stood up from the chair and we embraced in the way that good friends do, then with him sat on the bed and me back in the chair, he told me that he was having great difficulty coming to terms with my situation. He said that having known me for so long and what with me still only being a young man, he felt that it was a great waste of a life.

However, all that said, Alan confirmed that he had thought hard and long about Helen's telephone call and, although it would be very difficult for him emotionally, he felt that he would be able to find the strength to sort out the funeral for us. I said how grateful we both were that someone who knew us so well would taking over this responsibility from Helen; with that I stood up and embraced him once more. I asked Alan what he needed from us for him to proceed, but he said rather than rush things today, it would be better for Helen and me to discuss the finer details of the funeral arrangements when we were quietly on our own. We could then let him know what hymns and readings or any other requests we had. Helen said there was one thing she wanted to be sure of; Alan asked what it was, to which she replied that it was important for to her to know that we would eventually be buried together and whether he could locate a double burial plot for us at a graveyard somewhere. He asked if there was anywhere in particular we had in mind. Helen looked at me and held my hand and, with a nod from me she said that we were not overly concerned about the actual geographical location, just as long as it had some relevance to both of our pasts; she then quickly added that it also had to be on a hillside. This last point had always been essential for Helen and I had no reason to disagree. Alan said he would look into the situation regarding a double plot and get back to us as soon as possible and so with these weighty issues discussed and dealt with, Sue asked whether she should let the others back in. We nodded our confirmation and she went to find Andy to let him know.

Family and friends continued to arrive at the bedside and depart back to the Visitors' Lounge and conversations ebbed and flowed. Then sometime around mid-afternoon, Andy came to me and said that he had received a text from Kate, to say that she had landed safety in the UK and was now in a hire car heading towards the hospital. Helen was relieved and said to me that she just hoped that Kate was not too tired to drive safely for the onward journey.

Not long after receiving this news, Joyce and Albert [Mother and Father-in-Law] visited for the first time. This was particularly poignant for me, because after the deaths of my own parents many years before, I had kept in touch with them, almost as long distance surrogate parents, and kept them abreast of the progress of my own family with Christmas cards and the like. The pair of them had also been instrumental in getting Helen and I back together and Albert had told me in the past that he thought of me more as a son than a son-in-law, so these were the two people who, in the absence of my own Mum and Dad, I felt a great need to say goodbye to. I could see that it was going to be as hard for them as it was for me, so I asked Andy if we could have some privacy and he, again, held the visitors in the waiting room while we talked. Unfortunately, after twenty minutes or so, Joyce succumbed to the emotion of it all and so they decided to make a move home, saying that they would see me again soon. After they had departed, Helen opened another box of tissues and the conveyor of visitors resumed.

Sometime around 6.00pm, Andy came from the Waiting Room to tell us that Kate had 'just arrived' at the hospital, and that she would be with us once the ravages of the journey had been attended to, but I knew that our Kate did not 'just arrive' anywhere, she 'enters' and so it was, that after a gruelling 12,000 mile flight from the other side of the world, followed by a tiring 150 mile drive straight from the airport to the hospital, Kate 'entered' the room, resplendent in her perfect make up and beautifully coiffured hair. She swept round the foot of the bed arriving at my bedside and, being careful not to get her bag entangled in the NG tube, she bent forward and kissed me on the forehead and my heart gave up a smile.

However, the stresses of travelling so far, added to the emotion of being in the company of her mum and siblings for the first time in a couple of years, plus actually seeing me laying in the hospital bed, suddenly became too much for her. I could see tears well up in her eyes, she squeezed my hand and looked across the bed at Helen and then her tears brimmed over and small damp patches appeared on the bed cover. Andy instinctively understood that this was a close family moment and quietly asked the others in the room if they wouldn't mind giving us a few moments together. As they left, with Andy at the rear, he closed the door behind him, leaving the five of us together for the first time in a long time.

Kate was the first to speak and said how sad she was, that this terrible thing was happening to me and Helen while we were still only young. I took hold of Kate and Helen's hands, then asked them in turn to take hold of Jim and Alex's hands, and as we linked up in a circle around the bed I asked them, in a crackling whisper, to please be still for a moment because I had a few words I needed to say to them.

I looked at Kate, Alex and Jim, through a veil of tears and told them that yes, it was very sad that Mum and I would not grow old together as we had hoped we might, but that we were happy to have made the most of the time we had spent together, and in watching them grow into kind, caring adults with strong loving hearts. I said that they would now have to hold firm together, so that Mum could use their love as a solid foundation to build her life again after I had gone.

With this, Helen let go of Jim's hand and put her arms about my neck, she held her forehead against mine and the tears flowed freely all around. Then Kate, Alex and Jim took my right hand in turn and gave it a strong squeeze. Helen produced a flurry of tissues from the ever present box, and with eyes dabbed and noses blown, we made ourselves presentable for visitors again, but with the evening coming on, all those people who were not staying at the house overnight needed to get back home, ready for work the next day.

So one after another small groups of visitors came to say their goodbyes all trying, but mostly failing, to avoid them sounding permanent. It was a sad and sometimes difficult end to the day. People drifted away until there was just Helen and me left; she reached out and put her arms around my neck with her head on my chest, we held onto each other for the longest time and then, with a final kiss, she gently patted me on the chest and left.

Now that I was on my own, a melancholy came over me, but just as I felt it was about to overwhelm me there was a 'Ping!' from the direction of the over bed table. I pulled the table towards me and saw that there was a text message notification. I opened it and could see it was from my niece, saying that she was thinking of me, then another 'Ping!' - a text had arrived from Helen with love and kisses, and then 'Ping!' 'Ping!' 'Ping!' texts started arriving in quick succession, some letting me know that people had made safe journeys home and all sending their love. As quick as the melancholy had fallen on me, it was now lifted by the outpouring of love in these messages.

Knowing that there would be no atropine patches again tonight, I didn't bother to get into bed, instead I set the chair in place with pillows on the bed and after the nurse had been, I settled down in a much happier frame of mind and slept the better for it.

Monday 5ᵗʰ December

I was awake early and still sat in the chair from the night before, the curtains were closed and in the half-light my mind replayed the events of the weekend and the roller coaster of emotion that had enveloped me. It came to me in this moment that whatever uplift I had felt from the visits, it had done nothing to lessen the awfulness of my predicament. Christmas was now only three weeks away and I had already used up one of the weeks of life that had been on offer to me since the diagnosis, I could almost physically feel my life draining away.

The 'early' nurse did not find me very communicative and I was still sat in the chair when Helen and Kate arrived. I just couldn't be bothered with the effort of washing and shaving, but they both knew that I was due to have the MIR scan later on in the morning, so after some gentle persuading by Helen, I disconnected myself from my attachments and headed for the shower and, while Helen assisted me in my ablutions, Kate went off to get herself a cup of coffee.

By the time she returned, Helen had just about managed to craft me into someone prepared to meet the day ahead and in an effort to lighten my mood, Kate said that Mum had told her about my ice swallowing trick, which she thought was very clever of me, and could I show her how I did it. Not wanting a repeat of the previous water spillages, I asked Helen if she would get a towel and tie it bib-like, around my neck. I searched the water jug to find some small pieces of ice and then, to their sometimes difficult to control amusement, I proceeded to go through the awkward, but for me, rewarding process of getting small chunks of ice down my throat.

Having been able to repeat my little swallowing trick successfully for a new audience bucked me up slightly and this better mood was further boosted when Kate suggested that, rather than just plain ice, Mum might be able to freeze some fruit juice for me, so that I had some flavoured ice which would be nicer. Helen and I agreed that it sounded a good idea and so there then followed a detailed discussion on which fruit juice would be the best one to use. I said that I didn't think orange juice would be a good idea, because it tended to be quite thick and sometimes had bits in, and I worried they might catch in my throat when the ice melted. So it was agreed that it was going to have to be a choice of one of the berry juices, and in the end we all agreed that cranberry juice, which is a very clear juice, would be the best one to try. Decision made, Kate and Helen smiled, and said that this would be something to look forward to tomorrow, but it felt a bit odd to be told that I had anything to look forward to in my present situation.

It was then that the duty doctor came into the room on his daily rounds. He asked me if I was feeling tired after the weekend, because he had heard that I had received quite a few visitors. I said that it had been pretty exhausting, particularly as I had not been able to sleep very well due to the lack of atropine patches, which meant that I had to sleep in the chair next to the bed in order for me overcome my problem coughing. He raised his eyebrows in surprise and said that he would look into it, but if atropine patches were not available he would prescribe injections instead. He then checked my 'obs' chart and asked the usual questions about bowel movements etc., and once satisfied that things were as well as could be expected, he reminded us that the porter would be along shortly to take me for the MIR scan. He then put the 'obs' chart back and bid us good morning.

Helen said that she needed to replenish the things used up by the house full of visitors at the weekend, so when the porter came to collect me, she and Kate would nip over to the local supermarket to shop and come back to see me this evening, bringing Jim with them. Not many minutes later a porter arrived with a wheel chair. As I transferred into the chair I said I would rather be going to the supermarket with them than having an MIR scan. They smiled, said their goodbyes and waved cheerio as they left the room.

The porter wrapped a blanket around me and gave me my notes, which he told me to hold firmly on my lap. He then whisked me through the labyrinth of hospital corridors to where the MIR scanner was situated and I was once more left parked adjacent to the wall, waiting for the radiologist to come and get me. Luckily, it wasn't too long before a lady came introduced herself, she asked me whether I could walk into the room or did I need her to wheel me in. I said that I felt able to walk, so she took the notes from me and with me holding onto her arm, I shuffled into the scanner room.

This was generally a repeat of the previous CT scanner experience, except that this time, I was managing to control my swallowing more successfully, which meant that there was less interruption from my coughing. Happily, I managed the whole episode in one take, albeit the procedure had taken slightly longer than the previous time. Once the scan had been completed I was deposited in the wheelchair, back in my parallel parking spot next to the wall, waiting for the porter to arrive. There is a lot of waiting to be done in hospital.

Andy was waiting for me when I got back to the room, so after I was disgorged from the wheelchair back into the bedside chair and fully reconnected to my NG lifeline, I gave him a brief resume of how the MIR scan had gone. He wished me luck with the results and said he hoped they would throw more light on the problem. He went on to tell me that he had watched Matt and his dad, Tony, going through the company's files on the computer at home. He said that, where necessary, they had taken copies of the information Matt needed to run the business in the short term.

I thanked Andy for all his help in this matter and for all of his efforts over the weekend; he said that under the circumstances it was the least he could do. However, now that the weekend was over, he was going have to make tracks back home as he had to go to work the next day, but that he would keep in daily contact with both Helen and me and return next Friday bringing the family with him, unless of course things deteriorated in the meantime, in which case he would come back straight away.

After Andy had left, I spent the rest of the afternoon laid on the bed, watching a history channel on the TV, trying to fill the time until Kate, Helen and Jim arrived. The first thing they wanted to know was how the MIR scan had gone, I told them that I didn't know the results as yet, but that things had gone better than the previous CT scan, and so hopefully the consultant would get better information this time.

Helen deposited some clean clothes into the cupboard and Kate said that they had filled an ice cube bag with cranberry juice which was now in the freezer, ready for tomorrow. Jim, though, seemed fairly subdued; no doubt like the rest of us he was struggling to make sense of the situation we were all in, but it was more difficult for him with his exams looming large and there wasn't much I could give him in the way of encouragement or to say that things would get any better, I just hoped that he would manage to get by as he still had a future to prepare for.

After an hour or so of chatting, I was starting to feel the full tiring effects of the past couple of days and so, with reluctance, I said to them that I needed to rest and they agreed to leave so that I could get my head down.

The nurse arrived some time later, she had to wake me to give me my penicillin, diazepam and now also my atropine injections. I told her that I couldn't help but find it funny that she was having to wake me up to give me a sleeping potion, she smiled and explained that both of the penicillin and diazepam injections were intravenous and would be given through the cannula on the back of my hand. However the atropine injection was to be given subcutaneously. I had to ask what his meant and she said that the injection just went into the skin and not a vein. So after she had injected the first two into the cannula, she reached over to my right shoulder and pinched a small area of skin between her thumb and forefinger, and inserted the needle just under the fold in the skin. It did feel a little sore as the fluid was injected but nothing more than that.

I settled down on the bed again, the nurse turned the over bed light off and I started to drift away, my last waking thought was that I hoped that dying would be this comfortable.

Tuesday 6th December

I woke refreshed this morning instead of just coming to, as I had done following some of the recent disturbed nights; the atropine and the diazepam seemed to have done their jobs well. I can't say that I jumped out of bed and strode forth, but I did feel a slight spring in my step as I disconnected the empty feed bag and headed to the shower. I even had a go at cleaning my teeth with a toothbrush, well at least the ones you could see when I smiled.

I was sat in the chair and quite chipper when Helen arrived around 10.00am, so it was with some concern that I could see that she had been crying. I asked her what had happened, but she shrugged it off, so I just assumed that the situation must have been bearing down on her more heavily this morning.

Helen kissed me on the forehead and after taking off her coat, she reached into her bag and produced quite a handful of unopened envelopes. She said that having removed all of the dross from the post that she could, that these letters were either addressed to me personally or to the business and she wanted me to tell her what to do with the contents in case there were some bills that had to be paid, or things needed to be sent to Matt for him to deal with. I thought that it might be the added stress of having to deal with this, on top of everything else, that had made her cry, and so one by one I carefully went through them all with her, I felt at least I could do to try and put her mind at rest about this if not much else.

The business items were fairly easily dealt with, but some of the envelopes contained cards and letters that had been written by friends and family, protesting their disbelief at what was happening to me but finding it difficult to put their feelings of helplessness into words. We both sat there and intently read them all, some evoked an emotional response which needed time to overcome. Having finished reading, Helen helped me place the cards on the cupboard, I then explained to her the one or two items from the business correspondence that needed to be dealt with, which she noted down on her pad and this seemed to ease her worries a little.

Kate arrived just before lunchtime, she gave me a warm hug and then looking at Helen asked if I would mind her taking Mum to the hospital restaurant, Kate said she was concerned that Mum had not been eating properly. Helen protested, saying that she didn't want to leave me on my own when we had so little time together, and in any case she wasn't really hungry, but I persuaded her that she needed to keep her strength up and so she should go with Kate.

When they returned, I noticed that Helen was carrying one of her bag for life bags, which Kate must have brought in. She reached in and produced a small thermos flask and, while undoing the top, explained to me that before coming to visit, Kate had taken some of the cranberry juice ice cubes, put them in a plastic bag and crushed them with a rolling pin. Helen showed me the crushed pink ice in the flask, but before letting me at it, took a clean tea towel from the same bag and tied it around my neck. Kate said with a smile, that it was to save my clothes from any spillages, rather than use the previously commandeered hospital towels.

Fully prepared, Helen now pulled up a small chair and sat in front of me, she poured some of the crushed cranberry ice into the cup of the flask and with a spoon, which also appeared almost magically from the seemingly bottomless bag (*I remember thinking this girl thinks of everything*), she carefully put a small piece of ice into my mouth. The taste was glorious, but in my delight I swallowed it too quickly and immediately convulsed into a coughing fit. Score one to the tea towel.

The second attempt was more successful, and so we continued the process until most of the manageable sized pieces of cranberry ice had been consumed. I was elated because now I had taste, swallow and extra fluid, another small victory against the odds that put a smile on my face and set me up for the rest of the day.

We had just finished tidying things up when the consultant knocked and entered. I was sat in the chair and Helen and Kate moved away slightly so that he could perch on the edge of the bed next to me. He asked how I was feeling today. I said not too bad and explained about eating the cranberry ice. He thought this was a very good idea and was impressed at how Helen and Kate had organised it. He then gave a little cough and looked at Helen, the tone of his voice altered, and in an instant the mood in the room changed, we seemed to instinctively know that the conversation was about to move in a more serious direction and I noticed that Kate had moved towards Helen and was holding her hand.

The consultant said that he had seen the results of the MIR scan, and unfortunately they seemed to show, when compared to the result of the previous CT scan, that the cancer had got bigger over the previous seven days, and it now looked as though it was eating into the bone of the skull itself. I'm sure that my mouth must have dropped open and my eyes widened at this news, because he leaned forward and placed his hand on my right arm.

After a short pause he went on to explain that there is a hole where the nerves and blood vessels pass through the skull. This would normally be about the diameter of an ordinary pencil but the MIR images had shown that this hole was now nearly as big round as his finger, which he demonstrated by holding the little finger of his right hand between the thumb and forefinger of his left hand. Looking down at his hands I felt a sudden surge of heat pass through me, much like when you are angry or embarrassed, but I was neither. I just felt numb at this devastating development. I thought, "How can this be?" Surely I would feel the pain of the cancer growing in my head.

Helen let out a stifled cry; she let go of Kate and stooped down in front of me, almost at a kneel, and gripped both of my hands. She squeezed them tightly and then, standing up again, she faced the consultant and asked him if he was sure. With a subdued voice he replied, that from the scan images he had seen there was little doubt that things were getting worse, which bore out their previous diagnosis. He paused and then said that he was sorry that he could not hold out any better hope.

Helen's shoulders dropped noticeably and Kate moved close to support her; the consultant asked if there was anything he could do or get for us. Through the haze of my despair I heard Kate say there was nothing at the moment, and so he left, closing the door behind him on the way out. Kate remained standing as Helen moved to sit on the bed next to the chair, she gently pulled my shoulders towards her and cradled my head in her arms, and the three of us stayed in this unmoving tableau for what seemed quite a while.

I was the first to disturb the silence by saying that I needed a tissue to dry my eyes and blow my nose. Kate said that she would get it and disappeared into the shower room and even though she had her back to me, I could tell from the nasal tone of her throat clearing that she was in tears, which was made more obvious by her red ringed eyes when she came back into the room. I took the tissues from her and gave my nose a hearty blow and then, in a croaking whisper, I told them that, although bad, this was no different than we had been led to expect, which made it even more important for us to make the most of whatever time I had left. With that I stood up and we gathered together in a huddle and then spent the rest of the afternoon quiet reflection.

Towards the end of the afternoon, Kate said that she had run out of some of her toiletries and needed to go into town to get some more. She gave both me and Helen a warm hug and said that she would see me again later at visiting time.

Now that we were on our own, Helen's mood seemed to change; it was almost as though she had resolved something within herself and when she came and sat on the bed beside me, she spoke with a renewed assertiveness. Taking hold of my hand she looked straight at me and said that I had been right in saying what I had earlier, that we must make most of the time we had left. I nodded my agreement. Therefore, she continued, I want you to come home, where I can care of you for the rest of the time we have together. I was a bit taken aback by this turn of events and pulled my hand away. She quickly clasped it back and holding it more tightly said that we could arrange for the District Nurse or a Macmillan Nurse to help with any treatment needed. It would mean that I would have all my familiar things around me, and what's more, that I'd be able to sleep in our bed with her by my side.

Although I hadn't expected to have this discussion just yet, I had, during one of my sleepless moments alone in the dark, already given this matter some serious thought. I knew what I wanted to say to Helen, but also that it would come hard to her. So before saying anything, I looked to the ceiling for inspiration, but finding none there, I exhaled a deep sigh. Then, as gently as I could, I turned to her and told her that, although she knew how much I loved her and that she was the dearest thing in the world to me, I didn't want to go home to die. She looked hurt, as I knew she would, and she turned her face away. So I tried to explain, in words that couldn't, that my reason for saying this, was so she wouldn't be left with lasting memories which might cloud her judgement about moving on after I had gone. I said we both knew that she and Jim would not have the finances to continue living at the house, and that it wouldn't be fair on her emotionally, to find she had the need to sell but felt unable to, because of her last memories of me being there.

Helen looked at me again and tried to protest, but I remained firm and said that I thought the best thing would be to arrange for the hospice coordinator to come and see us and discuss what options there were, so with a sad reluctance she agreed to ask the duty doctor to set up a visit. Later, when she got up to leave, her goodbye lacked its usual warmth and I knew that I had upset her and I felt wretched as I listened to her footsteps fade into the distance down the corridor.

Not long after Helen had gone I saw the consultant pass by the corridor window. He opened the door and sat on the edge of the bed, close to where I was sitting in the chair. He said that he couldn't leave today without seeing how I was coping with the latest news. I said that it had really brought home the finality of the situation to all of us, but then his next comment took me by surprise when he said that although it would need to be agreed by the relevant people at the Birmingham hospital, there was one more thing that he would like to try. I looked at him intently and he continued by saying that he wanted me to have a PET scan (*Positron Emission Tomography*) to show exactly what the cancer was doing. I asked him what good it would do. He replied that he couldn't know in advance and it was probable that it would only confirm all of the previous tests;

however, the results might benefit others with a similar condition in the future.

This felt like one final straw was being offered to me, so I took hold of his wrist and in my croaky voice, I whispered that I didn't want him to give up on me and that if he could manage to sort out this cancer, I would work hard to sort out the paralysis. At this his expression warmed slightly, and he said he would do the best he could, although at this late stage of my condition it was unlikely that it would make any difference to my outcome. With that he said cheerio and that he would see me again on Thursday.

Once he had left, I texted Helen to say that they wanted me to go to a Birmingham hospital. 'Ping!' almost immediately a reply text in capitals blared NOW! I texted back and said, "No, I'll tell you about it later."

Helen, Kate and Jim arrived about 6.30pm, they could see that my demeanour had improved from earlier in the day, and so they gathered around me in the chair to hear what had happened. I explained as best I could what the consultant had said to me. I said that although it didn't necessarily mean that anything would change, it did seem to me that if they could find out more detailed information about the cancer, then with some kind of treatment or other, they might just be able to slow its growth down, which would at least give us a few more weeks together. Helen put her hand on my shoulder and smiled, and I could see the love in her eyes again.

Just then Alex and Ian arrived and were anxious to hear the new information, which once told made everyone feel a little bit happier. Helen asked me if I knew when I would be going to Birmingham and for how long, but I said that I wouldn't know until the consultant came back to me. However, it was my hope that whatever happened I could still have this room back when I returned.

Later, following a much happier visiting time and after the nurse had administered the contents due to me out of the drugs trolley, I tried to get some sleep, but I just couldn't settle, because my mind was still buzzing as a result of the day's seesaw ride of emotions.

Wednesday 7th December

Today I woke up before the 'early' nurse arrived, but having nowhere to go, there was no rush to get out of bed, and so I remained cocooned under the covers until after she had finished her morning routine and left. However, my duvet day was cut short by a pressing need to use the loo, so swinging my legs out of the bed, I disconnected the food pump, put on my dressing gown and headed for the shower room.

As I have previously explained, the mirror above the sink was a small, portrait shaped oblong in which I could only really see my head and shoulders and as I glanced in it, while washing my hands, I seemed to look my normal self, that is apart from the NG tube looped over my left ear so I was completely oblivious to any problem I might that might be brewing. On returning to the bedroom I sat in the chair, still in my night clothes, eagerly waiting for Helen to arrive, because she had promised to wash my back with the shower today, as it was something I was finding difficult to accomplish on my own.

She had only just entered the room and given me a kiss, when she suddenly stood back, and with a concerned look on her face asked what had happened to me. I raised my eyebrows and shrugged my right shoulder as much as to say I didn't understand what she meant.

Helen started pulling my dressing gown open so that she could see down the front of my night shirt and then pulled my head forward so that she could look around the back of my neck. She said that I was covered in blotches and asked me to stand so that she could lift my nightshirt up. When she did, I could see that my torso had what looked like a leopard skin pattern of dark red welts, and further investigation showed that the discoloration also covered the top of my thighs.

Checking still further, Helen pulled the leg of my underpants to one side, which exposed the even greater horror of an elongated blood blister in the crease of my right groin with an equally long blister on the other side, so with concern, bordering on panic, I asked Helen what she thought it might be. It was now her turn to shrug her shoulders and said that she would go and get a nurse to have a look at it.

When they got back, the nurse went through a similarly thorough investigation, before admitting that she didn't know what it was either, and turned on her heel to go and locate the duty doctor.

When the duty doctor arrived on the scene, with the nurse in tow, he was quick to understand the situation and stated, with some authority, that I had suffered a severe reaction to the large doses of penicillin I had been receiving, so much so that I had now become allergic to it. He said that he would contact my consultant to prescribe some different antibiotics for me and that, in the meantime, he would arrange for someone to come a couple of times a day and apply steroid cream which should help clear up the skin blotches and blood blisters.

Now that we knew what the problem was, the earlier panic subsided. However, we were still concerned at this latest development, particularly when the first thing that happened was that the nurse returned with a red wrist band, which she clipped onto my arm to warn others of my newly acquired allergy to penicillin.

Sure enough, about an hour later, someone did arrive to apply some cream. It was a very tiny man of Asian extraction who, apart from acknowledging us when he walked into the room, hardly spoke at all. I suspect this was mostly because he didn't much like the job he'd been given, but that apart, to give you some idea as to how diminutive he was, normally, when medics put on sterile gloves they have to stretch them to get them on, but on this chap they were as wrinkled as Nora Batty's stockings, and being no more than about 4'-3" tall in his stocking feet, the blue disposable polythene apron he was wearing, almost reached down to his ankles. He had brought with him two tubes of cream and so with very little conversation between us, he started applying their contents to the affected areas of my skin.

As she could see this was going to take some time, Helen said that she would like to go and catch up with some of her work colleagues to see how things were going in her department and to keep them abreast of what was happening to me, so I said that it was no problem and off she went.

It must have taken the tiny chap a good half hour or more to cover the affected areas in steroid cream, which was made all the more difficult for him because of my hirsuteness. When he had finished, he took off the apron and lobbed it, along with the spent gloves and empty tubes into the waste bin. As he was leaving the room I asked him what time he would be back, but because of my roupy voice he must have misheard me, because he nodded, smiled brightly and just said, 'Yes'.

So much for my promised back wash I thought, I now felt greasy all over and fed up with the day already, so I put my towelling robe back on, connected the NG tube back onto the food pump, switched it on and lay on the bed.

When Helen came back, I was surprised to see that she was accompanied by our solicitor; she had come across him in the corridor asking at the Nurses' Station for directions. He had just returned from holiday, so on the way to the room she had briefed him of the seriousness of my current condition. In the past our greetings had always been convivial, but obviously having been made aware that he was coming to assist me to draft a new will, his demeanour was quite formal and he approached the bed in a subdued manner saying how sorry he was that this was happening to me.

He sat in the chair and took a notepad from his briefcase. Helen sat on the edge of the bed and held my hand. I explained to him, that I had written a will around the time Helen and I had got married, some eleven years ago but that it was fairly irrelevant, now that my demise had been forecast within the next two to three weeks. I felt my knuckles being squeezed tightly and I tried to give Helen a reassuring look, but failed abysmally, and she dabbed at her eyes with a tissue.

I said to him that I just wanted a simple statement in the will leaving everything to Helen. He said that this wouldn't be a problem, but that we may be able to achieve some tax advantage, depending on how our property was divided between us. He said he would look into this and come back to see me after the weekend with a document for agreement and, if satisfied, my signature. I thanked him and he left.

Helen and I were both feeling deflated after having such a solemn discussion and rather than stay in the room and reflect on it, I asked her if she fancied another walk down the corridor. So still wearing my towelling robe and being careful not to stretch the NG tube, I pulled on some track suit bottoms and slipped my feet into my slippers and then, with my right hand pushing the wheeled drip stand and Helen supporting my left arm in the crook of hers, we once more stepped out into the corridor.

We shuffled on until we reached the double doors. Helen asked me whether I felt tired at all, but not wanting to return to the room just yet I said that I would like to wander a little further this time. Moving slowly on, we turned right into the adjoining corridor and on passing the Nurses' Station, one nurse looked up from her work and smiled; but although it was a friendly smile, it somehow seemed tinged with sympathy and I got the feeling that she knew she was looking at a dead man walking.

We arrived at the next set of double doors at the entrance to the ward, Helen stepped ahead and opened them so that I could shuffle through into the main corridor. I hadn't been this far from the room without being chauffeured by a porter in over two weeks, and it did feel that I was going on a bit of an adventure.

I could see to my left, that the corridor came to an end not too far away, and there were windows where we could see out and as I hadn't seen the world in general since my admission into hospital, I persuaded Helen to let us walk to the end of the corridor so that we could take in the view.

Our progress was slow, but eventually we arrived at the windows and as we looked out onto the world, things that we would not normally have taken much notice of, such as how people parked their cars or the number of seagulls that were flying overhead, seemed to take on an unusual significance and, from one particular angle, we could look along the side of the hospital to a high level canopy, which was a design feature of the building. I held Helen close and said that it reminded me of the time we had taken a cruise on the Oriana where, from our balcony, we could look along to the bridge of the ship. She agreed with me that there was a certain resemblance, and we spent a while reminiscing about the time we had spent on the cruise with Jim, who had been about six at the time. I reminded her that I had given her a china thimble for our 'cotton' wedding anniversary, and how each morning she had collected the sea salt which had crystallised onto the balcony rail overnight, she said that she still had the thimble at home wrapped in cling film.

Having rested enough to attempt the return journey, but in no particular hurry to get back to the room, we took our time retracing our steps. However, on rounding the corner into the corridor that led to my room, we could see the 'little man', in his blue gloves and disposable apron, standing in the distance, querulously looking this way and that. We looked at each other with an expression of faux surprise, as we suddenly remembered that I was due to have a second coating of steroid cream, so we tried to speed our shuffle and as we got close he told us that we needed to hurry, because he had left this to be the last job before he went home and he only had half an hour left now.

As he started slapping on the cream, Helen said that it was about time she went home and that she would see me later. So craning her neck in over the top of the little man who was now stooped in front of me, she gave me a kiss and left, smiling at the scene she was leaving behind. The 'little man' hurriedly applied the second coat of cream, and then quickly divesting himself of his protective garments into the bin in the corner of the room he left and I felt a twinge of jealousy that at least he could go home at the end of the day.

Evening visiting came and went and before she left Helen said that she would make sure to come in a bit earlier tomorrow, so that she could help me have a proper shower before the next cream application; I told her that I would look forward to it.

After they had gone I lay on the bed and watched some TV, to fill the time while I waited for the nurse to come and administer my drugs. Although I had earphones on, my attention was suddenly drawn to a loud clunk as the drugs trolley collided with the door frame, I looked across to see that it was not the usual nurse, and because of her different uniform I assumed that she must be an agency nurse and that was why she had misjudged the width of the door opening.

As she came near, to administer the new antibiotic and diazepam injections, I noticed a strong smell of tobacco smoke. This had happened once or twice before, and I had reckoned that some of the night nurses must nip out for a quick cigarette during their shift. However, tonight this nurse had the distinct sweet smell of an added smoking ingredient, with the open pupil stare of someone who is not able to focus on what they are doing and when she spoke it was quickly, in short excited sentences.

Having given the first two drugs into the cannula on the back of my hand, she came round the other side of the bed to administer the atropine injection. She took a pinch of skin on my shoulder, just like the nurse had done the night before, but rather than using gentle pressure, she drove the needle in quite hard, which made it feel a bit more sore than the previous night, but I didn't think a lot about it at the time. She then wiped the area of skin with a swab, tidied the syringes into the sharps box and left the room, still chattering away as she went.

I tried to get off to sleep, but I found that my throat started to clag up a bit more than it had done over the past couple of nights, which caused me to have a little clearing cough every so often, but eventually I must have drifted off.

Thursday 8th December

I was woken up by the noise of the 'early' nurse going through her usual routine, and I did feel rough, mostly from a lack of sleep, but also because I had a feeling of being unclean from not having had a shower the day before. However, I knew that Helen was going to come in early, to help me have a shower before the next application of steroid cream, so I just couldn't be bothered to move from the bed until she turned up.

Having arrived and having taken off her coat, she came towards the bed from the right hand side and started chiding me for being a lazy bones, but as she got close she gasped, "Oh! My God what have they done to you now?" Not having looked in the mirror yet this morning, my first thought was that she must be seeing some further manifestation of the recently acquired allergy to penicillin, but now she started tugging at the sheet under me trying to lift my right shoulder while, at the same time infected by her obvious concern, I twisted my head round to try and see what she was looking at, and there on the bed linen under where I had been laying was a large pink patch.

Baffled at what might have caused the stain, we decided that Helen should go and fetch a nurse who came hurriedly into the room to look at the problem. Helen watched as the nurse bent close and rubbed my shoulder, but we were both a bit bewildered when she left again without saying anything. Helen had another close look at my shoulder herself, and discovered what she thought looked like two puncture marks in my skin, apparently one entry and one exit.

From this we surmised, that last night, the nurse must have pushed the needle right through the pinch of skin, and emptied the content of the syringe directly onto the bed, then the resultant wound must have then bled a bit, which soaked into the wetted bed linen and coloured it pink. I said to Helen that this might explain why I had been coughing during the night.

It wasn't very long before the nurse came back, accompanied by a more senior colleague who closely inspected my shoulder and then, seemingly a little embarrassed, confirmed our earlier suspicion. She apologised and said that she would have to go and make a report of the incident but told me that, if I could get myself out of bed in the meantime, she would arrange for someone to come and change the sheets straight away. Helen and I later suspected that this was because she knew the consultant was due to visit and didn't want him to see the evidence.

All I wanted was to get properly washed and shaved before the next coating of steroid cream so, with Helen's assistance, I made my way to the shower room, and while the bed changing team completed their task, I shaved myself and was scrubbed up fresh as a daisy, just in time for the little man in his blue plastic pinny and gloves when he came to recoat me. Helen smiled and said that rather that watch me being turned into a butterball again she would go and get herself a cup of tea.

While she was away the consultant called in to see me. At the time I had only been coated on one side, so working his way carefully around the cream applicator extraordinaire, the consultant picked up my notes and satisfied with what he saw, he looked at me and said, that the request for me to have a PET scan had been put forward to the management team in Birmingham and that they would make a final decision on Friday or, at the very latest, the following Monday, which would mean that I could then be moved to Birmingham on the Tuesday. I thanked him for coming to let me know, and he carefully eased himself back around the diminutive nursing assistant and left.

The last of the cream had just been rubbed in when Helen came through the door. She was carrying one of those insulated cardboard cups and, while she sat in the chair and sipped her tea, I put on my towelling robe and told her of the consultant's visit and said that all being well, I could be going to Birmingham on Tuesday. Helen said that she was pleased, but I said to her that I was already starting to have doubts about the move; firstly, because if it achieved nothing I would have left this nice private room for a large hospital ward which would not be as pleasant a place to end my time and secondly, it would be a lot more difficult for Helen to visit because of the 150mile round trip. Helen, always looking for the positive side of things, said that anything that meant we might have more time together would be worth trying and, in any case, with the help of family and friends, she was sure that the travelling would not prove too much of a problem. So in the end we agreed, that if the Birmingham hospital accepted the request for the PET scan I would go for it and see where it led.

The duty doctor looked in through the corridor window and seeing that we were on our own he came into the room. He said that he had managed to get in touch with the Hospice Coordinator who, on hearing about my life expectancy, had rearranged her diary so that she could come and see me the next morning, probably around 11.00am. He asked Helen whether she could be at the meeting as well. She replied that it would not be a problem and thanked him for his efforts.

Receiving the information soured our mood somewhat, particularly as we knew that Alan (P) would be returning at the weekend and we had promised him the details of the funeral arrangements. It was a subject that we had skirted around several times but had never managed to finalise, partly because it was so upsetting and partly because it made the actual event seem so real. However, I didn't want Helen to have to deal with the task after I had died, so although it would be a difficult matter to discuss, I knew that it was better dealt with while I was still fully compos mentis and that it could only be done when we were on our own. I tentatively broached the subject once more with Helen, who although reluctant, knew it had to be done and so she came and sat on the bed beside me.

Reaching into her handbag Helen pulled out her writing pad and placed it on her lap, as she sat up I put my arm round her shoulder and she let out a deep sigh. We made a start, but just having to write Funeral Arrangements at the top of the page made it difficult for her right from the off. Emotions contained, we moved on.

The first item to be listed was where to hold the funeral. Helen said she would like the service to be carried out at the village church so that the people we knew locally could come to say their goodbyes. I agreed, but said that the one thing I didn't want was to have a vicar, who I had never met, repeating to everyone at the funeral, the few facts that he had managed to glean from her, and putting them across as though he had known me for a long time. I said to her that as Alan had already said he would speak for me, that this item was easily settled.

The next items on the list were whether there would be any readings and what music I wanted to be remembered by. Helen wrote down the details as we discussed them and then, placing the pad and pen on the bed, she turned and put her arms around my shoulders and through her sobs she whispered, "Thank you."

In this current mood of reflection I felt that I needed to make some kind of gesture, possibly a lasting physical reminder of me for her to keep into the future, but what?

I gently took hold of her hand and in that moment of tenderness a thought came to me. I put it to her that she might like to have a lock of my hair. Her hand tightened on mine and, with eyes wet with tears, she was unable to respond save for a trembling smile and nod of her head. I said to her that being the case, it would make me the happiest if she received it as a living gift rather than have her take it from my cold body. We embraced, and with her head on my shoulder she said quietly, that she would bring in some scissors when she visited later with Kate and Jim.

Before she left I realised, that in all the morning's hullabaloo regarding the stained bed sheets, I hadn't had the cranberry ice. We found the flask lying in the bottom of her carryall bag, but on removing the top we could see that it had all melted. Expressing my disappointment, Helen said she would see if there was any left in the freezer at home and bring it back with her that evening.

Once more on my own, I decided to try and get some rest after the fractious sleep of the previous night. I was just beginning to doze off when I was abruptly woken by a loud noise. I looked towards the door and could see that a large trolley had crashed into the double doors, which spanned the corridor just outside my room. Wanting to know what had happened, I rolled over to see that two of the porters had tried to push a strange looking bed trolley through the doors, but that something must have been on the other side which prevented them. The trolley looked like a normal bed except that it had a box arrangement on the top, with a solid metal top and canvas sides. I watched them, as they muttered with obvious frustration, while manoeuvring the trolley backwards and forwards, but after a bit of to-ing and fro-ing they finally managed to sort themselves out and continue their journey through the doors.

Excitement over, I turned on my side again with my back to the door and I was just getting settled when another knock brought me up with a start. Feeling slightly annoyed at being disturbed again, I rolled onto my back, but this time, framed in the doorway, I could see the familiar figure of someone I knew from our village.

After living in rural Herefordshire for a number of years, I had found that many small villages seemed to have an incumbent retired professional, someone like a banker or military person, who by general consensus, tended to evolve into the unelected de facto mayor and here was ours. Bespectacled, well spoken, a keen gardener and genuinely interested in village matters and today dressed as every bit the country gentleman in a pair of corduroy trousers and a tweed jacket with the obligatory leather patches on the elbows. He had his cap rolled up in his hands like a baton, which made his knuckles go white. I beckoned for him to come in and pointed towards the chair, but he did not sit at first and stood some way from the bed.

In a less than firm voice, he said that since hearing of my illness, many of the villagers had made contact with him and because they did not want to bother Helen at this difficult time, they had wanted, through him, to let us both know that we were being thought of and prayed for; also to find out if there was any way in which they could be of help and so he had come along today, on behalf of the village, to see what could be done. I thanked him and again motioned for him to sit in the chair, which he did.

I managed, in my hoarse whisper, to say that I was very grateful for his visit and asked him to relay my and Helen's thanks to everyone for their concern. Then it came to mind that he was one of the church wardens, so I said that in fact there was something that he might be able to help us with, to which he replied that he would do his best. I told him that it was Helen's wish to have my funeral service at our local church but, because neither of us were church members, we were not sure if this could happen and, knowing that he was one of the church wardens, whether he might be able to assist. He said that he felt sure that it would not be a problem.

Being relieved at freeing myself of one worry, I told him that there was also another matter which was giving me concern. He asked how he could help. I said that at some future period, our house would have to be put on the market, and although Helen would probably not ask for it herself, I would be grateful if he could rally the villagers to help her pack up the house because it would be a considerable task for her on her own. He gave me his assurance that he would see to it and I thanked him, saying that it had taken a great weight off of my mind. I asked him again if he would pass on my thanks in advance for any help that the villagers gave to Helen in the future.

He said that he would, then getting up from the chair he reached out and shook my hand in farewell and, as he turned to leave, I saw him take a hanky out of his trouser pocket, so that he could rub his eyes and, on leaving the room, I heard him blow his nose, loudly, while the clicking of the metal heels on his shoes slowly faded into the distance as he walked away.

Time had moved on, and although I could really have done with some sleep, my evening visitors were starting to arrive. However, almost as if by means of reward for my stoicism, Kate had managed to find some cranberry ice left in the freezer, so in order for me to enjoy the treat, I moved from the bed into the chair and, having been suitably adorned with tea towels to protect against the inevitable coughing fit, I was pleased to be able to perform my ice swallowing trick to this somewhat captive but appreciative audience.

Despite the encouragement, I soon got tired from the exertion and had to move back onto the bed to rest. Once settled, I told Helen about my afternoon visitor. She said how nice it was of everyone to be thinking of us and that she was pleased I had broached the subject of funeral arrangements with Ron. I then remembered the earlier commotion in the corridor, but when I told Helen about it, her expression tensed as she explained that some poor soul must have passed away on one of the wards and it would have been the porters using the mortuary trolley. It was proving difficult for us to keep our spirits up for any length of time, when the finality of death was always around us.

As the evening visiting came to a close, Kate and Jim said that they would leave us alone for a while. Once they had gone, Helen produced a small pair of scissors and a short length of what turned out to be embroidery wool from her bag, she asked me where she should take the lock of hair from, I smiled and said that it didn't matter to me, but preferably not a grey bit. Then gently taking hold of a small amount of my hair between her thumb and forefinger, she tied it securely with the length of wool and started to cut with the scissors, I could feel the crunching as the blades severed each strand of hair.

Having completed the deed Helen showed me the result. I took it from her in my right hand, kissed it and then gently laid it in the open envelope she held in front of me, which she then closed and placed back in her bag, along with the scissors. We held each other for what seemed the longest time and then, with a slow, sad parting, she left to take the others home.

I was still in low spirits when the drugs trolley was trundled into the room. However, it cheered me a little to see that I had a different nurse to administer the injections and, once done, it did not take long for me to get off to sleep.

Friday 9ᵗʰ December

I have always said, if the sun comes up and you're still breathing, then you have to do another day and this morning felt like today could be a struggle. I wasn't looking forward to the meeting with the lady from the hospice, or the unpleasant dual coating of steroid cream, so I had a less than happy head on when Helen arrived.

We drudged through my ablutions with little conversation between us and then, having dressed, I sat in the chair, still unable to shift my sullen mood. Helen tried to move things along a bit, by producing another tranche of letters from her bag, but I just couldn't rally any interest and petulantly threw them, unopened, onto the top of the cupboard and my mood didn't improve any, when the diminutive vision in blue arrived to execute the first cream application of the day.

I sat there in grim silence while he did his work so Helen, realizing that she couldn't perk me up, said that she would go and get herself a cup of tea and come back later for the hospice meeting, but directly she had left the room I felt guilty. Deep within me I knew that I had let my own vexations come between us, and that Helen was having to bear far more than her fair share of the emotional burden that was piling down on us. I desperately wanted her to come back quickly so that I could apologise, but she made her cup of tea last a long time and did not return until just before the lady from the hospice was due.

When she came into the room I could see that she had been crying, so I got off of the bed and tried to close the distance between us as quickly as I could. I held her close with my right arm and told her how deeply sorry I was for upsetting her. She put her hand gently on my chest and lifted her head to kiss me, saying that she couldn't imagine the turmoil I must be going through and, in that moment of her compassion, my crabbiness fell away.

At the appointed time there was a knock at the door. Helen and I looked at each other tentatively and then she called for the visitor to come in. A smart looking lady entered the room and introduced herself; we could see that she was middle aged with dark hair and dressed in a white blouse with a dark jacket and skirt. She pulled a chair up to the end of the bed, sat down and took a pad and pen from her briefcase.

She first asked us whether we knew of the hospice movement and what it did. We said that we had a vague idea, so continuing in a manner which we found reassuring, she proceeded to explain what her role was and how the hospice system worked. It wasn't long however before the topic got round to the end game, and she asked me why I had chosen to apply for a place at the hospice, rather than spend my last days at home. I explained that Helen was actually in favour of the latter, but that I felt strongly that it would not be a good thing, and set out my reasons, which she said that she could understand.

I then told her of my concern that if I was sent to the Birmingham hospital and things deteriorated quickly, would it still be possible for me to come back to the local hospice so that I could end my days closer to my family? She said that it shouldn't be a problem. I thanked her saying that it took a great weight off of my mind to know that agreeing to have the PET scan would not close the door of the local hospice to me.

We then got onto the details of palliative care, and what the closing stages of my life might be. I said to her that all I was really interested in was having enough pain killing drugs available, so that the ending could be as painless as possible, for both me and my family. However, I said, of equal importance to me was that as far as was possible, I wanted to have some dignity in the process of dying. She assured us both that was exactly what the hospice system of care was intended for.

She handed Helen some leaflets about the hospice, and told her that we could contact her at any time. She said that there wouldn't be any problem with my having a place at the hospice and that we shouldn't worry, because she would keep in touch with the hospital to monitor how things were progressing. We thanked her for coming to see us at short notice; she smiled and said that it was all part of her job.

After she had gone, Helen and I agreed that the visit had been a lot less harrowing than we had been expecting, and it was good to know that no matter how bad it might get, there were people who knew exactly what to do, and they were going to be there to support us both right up until the end.

Helen said that she needed to get some bits in for the folk who would be visiting me and staying over at the house for the weekend, so rather than return home now and come back this evening, she would call in to see me when she had finished shopping and then she could be at the house when people arrived, and off she went.

While she was away, and probably because it was POETS day, the second application of cream was completed by early afternoon and, what with the weekend visitors due to arrive and my transfer to the Birmingham hospital looming large, the times when Helen and I could be private were very precious, so I was really hoping that when she did return there wouldn't be any interruptions for the rest of the afternoon.

Luckily that was the case, and we spent a happy time reminiscing about all the walks we had done when we first moved to Hereford. It had been our ambition to climb to the top of all the high spots around where we lived, so that we could look back and try to spot the house, a task made slightly easier by the very tall Wellingtonia tree which was situated in the small piece of adjacent woodland. I had always joked that one Christmas I would stick some lights on it and fix a big flashing star at the top.

However, as the afternoon went by it became more and more difficult to avoid the awful truth of what lay ahead of us, and we found our discussions wandering through both real and surreal subjects: an effect that impending death seemed to be having on our minds, and there was one such subject that I knew I needed to deal with.

I had no doubt that after I was gone, family and friends would rally around and look after Helen, but nevertheless I saw it as an important task, in the time left to me, to make my passing as easy as I could for her. My main concern was that I didn't want her to feel she had to spend the rest of her life on her own as a lonely widow. It was a very difficult subject to broach and I have to say that I made a real ham fist of it.

During the course of our conversation, I reached for her hand and she turned to look at me. I told her of my concern for her future and suggested that I should set her free of her marriage vow, so that in the future she would always know, that I had been comfortable with the thought of her sharing her life with someone else. How wrong could I have been? She pulled her hand sharply away, and with firm, disparaging comments she let me know, in no uncertain terms, that this was not an offer she had either wanted or asked for. She said that for her, there would be no-one else, and to emphasise her disapproval she moved away from me, and didn't say anything for quite some time.

It was Helen who eventually broke the silence, by saying that it was not the thought of death itself, which gave her the greatest upset, it was that her sleepless nights were constantly invaded with the nightmare of not being able to find me again on the other side. She said that it had always been her hope that, when we died, it would be together but now she was worried that she wouldn't know how or where to find me when it came to be her turn.

Desperate to hunt down an answer to her torment, I said that I remembered from a reading, which I had done for a friend's daughter's wedding, that only three things could last forever: they were faith, hope and love and that the greatest of these was love. I said we knew our love was strong, and that if we held fast to it we would always be able to find each other. I then reached around the edge of the bed, making a play of first trying to find and then tying an imaginary cord around both my waist, and then hers, I told her it was an everlasting golden cord of love, which could stretch forever and that, if she kept the knot tied, she would be able to find me no matter how far I had travelled on the other side. I pretended to test the knot by stretching the cord between us and then, following my example, Helen did the same. Almost on cue the sun came out, and a reflected warm glow from the red brickwork shone into the room.

Although this had lifted our mood, Helen still looked very drawn and tired from her lack of sleep, so I asked her to lay on the bed beside me. At first her hospital training made her a bit reticent, but I managed to persuade her that it would be OK, and after drawing the curtains to the corridor window, she sat on the edge of the bed, kicked off her shoes and lay back. Fortunately hospital beds are reasonably wide, so we were able to lie side by side in a foetal position, and it wasn't long before she fell sound asleep. This was the closest we had been, as man and wife, for nearly two weeks, and although all I could do was drape my paralysed left arm over her, I was just happy to be holding her close again.

I was enjoying this rare moment of closeness, so I was quite exasperated to hear a quiet knock at the door. The door opened, and Gordon's face tentatively peered around the jamb. I didn't want to speak, because I was determined that Helen's sleep should not be disturbed. However, unable to use my useless left arm I couldn't wave him away, so I gently lifted my head from the pillow and slowly shook it from side to side, hoping that he would get my silent message. Luckily he caught on straight away and ducked back out of the room, closing the door quietly after him. I felt a bit guilty about Gordon, this was his second attempt to visit and he had been unsuccessful on both occasions.

The late afternoon sky slowly lost its brightness, there were no lights on in the room, and the curtains filtered the corridor lighting, so the room gradually became a dark, quiet, warm cocoon and Helen continued to sleep soundly.

She eventually woke about 5.30pm; she turned her head sleepily towards me and smiled warmly, but when she realised what the time was she said that she was surprised that I had let her sleep so long. I told her that I had not wanted to disturb her any earlier, both because of my enjoyment at having her so close, and knowing that she needed the sleep.

A little concerned that folk would be arriving at the house for the weekend and that they would be tired and hungry after their journeys, she said that she thought she had better get home, and I grudgingly agreed. She rolled her legs over the side of the bed and slipped her feet into her shoes, she stood up and put on her coat, and then leaned over the bed to kiss me goodbye, but as she left the room she remembered the imaginary cord we had tied earlier, and made a play of giving it a big tug. I lifted my hip in response, pretending that I could feel her pulling on the other end, at which she smiled, winked her eye and then disappeared from view but, unlike my usual despair at us parting, I felt somehow uplifted, that we had seemed to reconnect in some way.

About an hour after Helen had left, Andy and Sue called in briefly on their way to the house. He told me that there would be quite a few people coming again this weekend. I said to him that I of course was very grateful to them, but because I had no idea how much more time Helen and I would have together, particularly after I was moved to the Birmingham hospital, what I really wanted most of all was to spend as much time as possible with her. He said that he understood and that he would try to pace the visits in order that we could have our own space as well.

It had been a long emotional day which, thankfully, came to a close much better than it had started out, so I was quite happy to have my medication and get some sleep ready for the weekend ahead.

Weekend - Saturday 10th and Sunday 11th December

This Saturday started much as the last one had, with the hospital coming noisily into life after the night-time lull and, as this was going to be the last weekend that I would be able to say goodbye to the folk who could make it to Hereford hospital, I wanted to make sure that I looked my best so, after disconnecting the NG tube from the food pump, I headed for the shower room. On the way I checked my mobile and having clicked through the good night and good morning texts I found one from Helen saying that she would soon be on her way, so after a dodgy shave, a tricky shower and a messy attempt at dental hygiene, I applied some deodorant, got dressed, combed my hair and waited for her to arrive, quite pleased at the results of my one armed ablutions.

When Helen arrived, I could see as soon as she came into the room that her thoughts about the day ahead had matched my own. She had on a dress that she knew I liked her to wear, her hair had a real bounce to it, and as she came close she was preceded by the scent of her best perfume. A short time later Andy came and took post marshalling the visitors, who arrived in and departed from my room in small groups of three or four.

Some visits proved more traumatic than others; a lot of tears were shed, and, on more than one occasion, a very strange thing happened. As a group of visitors were leaving the room, one would hang back. They would come close to me, hold my hand and say something like, how on earth had things come to this or, how terrible it was that I had such a short amount of time left. Then totally unexpectedly they would go on to say, usually in a low voice, that they needed to tell me something and proceed to confide some secret from their past and tell me that it was the first time they had told anybody. It was almost as though they were trying to use me as a confessional, hoping that following my imminent departure to the hereafter, I might be able to obtain some kind of absolution for them. It was a discomforting burden.

Later on in the afternoon Alan and Sue arrived, and so that Helen and I could have a private discussion with them about the funeral arrangements, Andy corralled the other visitors in the waiting room for a while.

Alan told us that his enquiries had managed to locate a double burial plot, on a hillside, in a cemetery just outside Winchester, which he thought would fulfil our requirements and that he had the paperwork with him so that we could make an application to purchase it. Helen was holding my hand, and I could feel her shudder at the finality of the decision we were being asked to make, so I thanked Alan but said that before signing we would take the forms and read them later. Helen turned and smiled at me; she squeezed my hand before letting go, so that she could retrieve her notepad from her bag. We then spent some time discussing the funeral arrangements which Helen and I had agreed earlier in the week.

Alan said that he had already checked with the Church Wardens, who had confirmed that the funeral could be held at the local church, just as Helen had wanted. However, he was concerned that the long journey to Winchester would be too much to attempt on the same day and that his recommendation was for a small family group to escort the coffin on the long journey to the interment, a day or so later. I had a bizarre, momentary thought flash through my mind. Where would I spend the time in between and what I would do while I was waiting? But I held back from giving voice to my somewhat surreal concerns so as not to upset Helen.

Sue took copious notes of our discussions, but on seeing the strain that talking about the funeral was having on Helen and I, she suggested that the small details could be finalised later. Alan agreed saying that they should probably be making tracks anyway. He said that on their way out he would let Andy know not to let anyone else visit for a while to give us time to collect our thoughts. We thanked them both for all their efforts on our behalf, Alan said that it was the least they could do under the circumstances.

For us, each day that passed by was bringing the end of everything we held dear ever closer, which was being emphasised by all the fiscal, funerary and legal planning we were having to cope with so it took us some time to compose ourselves ready to receive more visitors.

By early evening I had become very tired; the remaining family visitors had said their goodbyes and Andy and Helen were the last to leave. I shook Andy's hand and we both thanked him for giving us the space we needed during the day, he then waited outside the door while Helen made sure that I was comfortable in bed before kissing me goodnight.

Sunday pretty much continued in the way that Saturday had left off, but the real blessing of the weekend for me was that no little man came to cover me in steroid cream and, in fact, the blotches from the penicillin allergy were already fading quite noticeably.

Several people made return visits; some had stayed at the house overnight, while others lived locally in the surrounding area, and I was pleased to see Joyce and Albert again. Joyce, in particular, found the visit much less traumatic than she had the previous one.

As the day came to a close I was left with many thoughts of the kindnesses everyone had shown over the weekend, their concern for Helen and the rest of the family. I felt humbled and blessed to have such loving people around me, but the realization that they had come to say their last goodbyes set my mind into a fearful overdrive about what may lie ahead during my last few days, so by the time the nurse arrived with the drugs trolley, I really needed the diazepam to calm me down.

Monday 12th December

A strange sight confronted me as I got ready to shower - my skin had started to peel over most of the trunk of my body. I guessed that the fact I was beginning to resemble a half plucked chicken was down to the many steroid cream applications I had received over the past few days. However, the good news was that the red blotches and blood blisters were now almost gone.

The second thing that I noticed, when I looked in the mirror over the wash basin, was that my ears seemed to be sticking out more than usual. At first, unlike the peeling skin, I couldn't think what might be causing this but then I remembered that a similar thing had happened to me once before. It was at the time, about fifteen years earlier, when I had gone through a divorce and because of one thing and another, I had lost a lot of weight. It dawned on me that I must be losing weight again, due to my only receiving sustenance from the NG food. Well, I thought, at least now I won't be such a heavy weight for the pall bearers to carry.

Once I had got ready for the day, I sat in the chair and switched on the TV, to while away the time until Helen arrived. I plugged in the earphones and thought that I would flick through the channels to see if any of the history channels had anything to offer. I was pressing the buttons when the screen suddenly filled with a shot, probably taken from a helicopter, of a massive fire with a huge plume of black smoke streaking across the countryside; transfixed, I listened to the reporter's voiceover. They were explaining that it was the aftermath of an oil tank explosion at a place called Buncefield; evidently a huge fire had started the day before. I thought to myself that it was funny no-one had mentioned it. The news reporter went on to say that although several people had been taken to hospital there had been no casualties and that several teams of fire fighters were still on the scene trying to put out the fire.

I had previously been avoiding television news programmes, mainly due to the fact that I didn't want to get involved with a story line that I may not get to see the end of. However, as a qualified health and safety consultant, the pictures triggered my inherent desire to know how and why this disaster had occurred. So it was much to Helen's surprise that she found me glued to the newscast when she arrived and, in fact, I didn't really notice her until she had circled the bed and arrived at my side. She nodded over my shoulder and I turned to see that Kate was with her as well but had stayed at the end of the bed.

I took off the headphones and Helen kissed me on the cheek. I flicked the switch to turn the TV off, and said that I hadn't heard about the fire that had started the previous day. Helen replied that she hadn't either until she arrived home when it was all over the TV news. Kate confirmed that it had happened early in the morning and a lot of nearby homes and businesses had been seriously damaged but, thankfully, no-one had been killed or seriously injured.

After taking off her coat Helen took a small pile of post from her bag which we opened and went through together. However, there was nothing that needed urgent attention so she collected up the dirty clothes to take home to wash and folded them into a carrier bag while Kate assisted me with the flask of broken ice, which today was blueberry flavoured.

It must have been about 11.00am when the solicitor arrived. He had with him my last will and testament ready for me to sign but informed me that my signature would need to be witnessed by a notary or other suitable person and he suggested that the hospital office manager would have the necessary gravitas and so he went off to locate her. While he was away Helen and I took the opportunity to have a good look through the document he had brought so

Kate said she would leave us to it and go and get a cup of coffee.

It was a good twenty minutes or so before the solicitor returned to the room, unaccompanied. He told us that he had managed to locate the Office Manager and she had said that in the circumstances she would be happy to act as a witness but, unfortunately, she was just about to go to an important meeting and could not assist until the meeting was over which would be in about an hour's time. The solicitor, not wanting a long wait at my bedside, said that he had some other things he needed to do back at the office so he would nip off and pop back in an hour's' time to get the document signed.

By this time Kate had returned, bringing with her a cup of tea for Helen and while we sat chatting there was a knock at the door. I recognised the person standing there as a senior member of my Masonic Lodge so I beckoned him to come into the room. After general introductions to Kate and Helen, he said that as it was the new Master's Installation meeting that evening, he thought that he would come along to see how I was holding up and to find out if there was anything that I needed so that he could report the matter back to the Brethren. With all that had gone on over the past week I had completely forgotten that this big occasion was happening today.

I thanked him for his concern but said that, apart from assisting Helen in the future, I couldn't think of anything that was pressing at the moment. I explained to him that there was the possibility of my going to the Birmingham hospital the next day and said that, although I wouldn't expect anyone from the Lodge to drive such a distance to visit me, they would be very welcome, particularly if it was to assist Helen with the driving.

He said he had no doubt that people would be willing to drive Helen and the family to Birmingham if requested, and then just as he was leaving he seemed to have a thought. He turned and asked me if there was anything I would particularly like to be said on my behalf during the toast to absent Brethren at the festive board.

This caught me a bit by surprise, so I thought for a minute and then said that I couldn't think of anything for anyone to say but the one thing that I desired most, but was unable to achieve, was to have a drink of water and that maybe in memory of me, the Brethren might like to drink the toast with a glass of water rather than wine. He said he thought that it would be a nice gesture and was sure the Brethren would be happy to do so.

An hour had just about passed when the solicitor returned; he said that on his way in he had checked on the whereabouts of the Office Manager but, unfortunately, the meeting had gone on longer than expected and therefore there was nothing to do but wait until she was free to come to the room.

So we waited. However, it was difficult to make polite conversation about a will and so, in between some pregnant pauses, we talked about the solicitor's recent holiday, the state of the weather - not that I had had much recent personal knowledge of it - and everyone's surprise at how amazing it was that no-one had been killed in the explosion at the oil storage depot. Then Helen remembered to ask after the health of the solicitor's wife and Kate answered some of his questions about her new life in New Zealand. Then luckily, as we desperately tried to search for a new topic of conversation, there was a knock at the door. A lady dressed in a smart suit entered the room, she was carrying a file in the crook of her arm and she expressed her apologies for the delay.

The solicitor having now waited for some time and obviously eager to get away, sprang to his feet and moved the over bed table to a position where I could sign the document. He explained to us the significance of what we were about to do and after we had all nodded our understanding of the situation he produced a pen from his inside breast pocket which he handed to me so that I could sign first, followed by the Office Manager and, as quickly as that, the whole of my worldly possessions were pledged to another.

Signing complete, the solicitor swiftly gathered up the document and placed it in his briefcase. I thanked him for his help and we shook hands. He seemed to lower his eyes a little as he said goodbye to me, probably knowing it would be the last time we would see each other, then Helen and Kate both thanked him and he and the Office Manager left. I thought to myself, well, that's another nail in the coffin completed.

The finality of what had just happened bore down on Helen who had tears in her eyes as she held my hand and I could see that Kate was upset as well. She dabbed at her eyes with a scrunched up tissue and said she could do with hot drink. I said if she waited a minute or two the tea lady was due and I was sure that she would be kind enough to let them have a cup of tea.

Helen said that the tea lady had been a great friend to us over the last couple of weeks, it was she who had provided the cup of tea for the abortive extreme tea drinking episode and, even though she knew that I was NIL BY MOUTH, she called in twice a day, every day, except the weekends, to say hello. She always had a bright smile and kind word and, if ever she saw that Helen was visiting at the time, she would always offer her a cup of tea with a biscuit and when we told her that I could swallow cold things she would go out of her way to get a small paper covered block of ice cream from the kitchens, the type we had been given at parties years before as children. I said to Helen that I would really miss the tea lady in her brown gingham tabard when I changed hospitals. She replied that there were bound to be tea ladies at Birmingham hospital, but I said that they wouldn't be the same.

Before they left for the day, Helen told me she had a long standing appointment in the morning, which she really ought to attend. However, Jim had the day off college so he would keep me company the next day until she arrived. I said that would make a change and asked if she thought he would remember to bring in the flask of fruit ice. Helen smiled and said that she would leave a stickit on the fridge door to remind him.

About midway through the evening, I was sat in the chair, catching up on the latest information on the oil fire, when there was a knock at the door and the consultant came into the room, which was a bit of a surprise this late in the day. I pulled the off the earphones and pushed the TV to one side and he came and sat next to me on the bed. He said that he had called in on his way back from the Birmingham hospital because he wanted to let me know personally, that the result of the meeting in Birmingham had not gone in my favour. It had, unfortunately, been decided that because my prognosis was so poor, it would not make sense to authorise a PET scan on the basis of cost against outcome. Evidently, at this late stage of my condition, it had been felt that having one would not lead to any beneficial treatments that could extend my life expectancy.

My heart sank and my head drooped into my hand.

The consultant put his hand on my shoulder and assured me that he was not prepared to give up so easily. He said that he knew of a patient who was due to be discharged from the ward at Birmingham sometime the next day and that, if I agreed, he would send me there 'on spec' so to speak, because he knew that he could argue my case better if I was on site at Birmingham rather than stuck here in Hereford. He said that I would need to be ready to move sometime in the early afternoon once the discharge of the other patient had been confirmed.

I felt that this was the worst case scenario for me. I knew that I could not expect Helen to visit me so frequently in Birmingham, and I already had misgivings about foregoing my private room for an open ward, particularly at a time when my condition was due to deteriorate further and there was a definite likelihood of me becoming incontinent. All the horrors that this would hold for me stacked up as a huge negative against the slim positive that the PET scan may, just may, offer the hope of a treatment which, if successful, might allow me to spend a small amount of extra time with Helen even though that would, in all likelihood, be at the hospice.

It was a surprisingly difficult decision for me to make, but I remembered what I had said to Andy back at the start of all this: about me being prepared to undergo treatment if it would give me more time with Helen, just as long as I could die with some dignity. So I lifted my head to face the consultant and said that I would place my trust in him. If he thought that there was even the slimmest chance that the PET scan could offer a better insight into the cancer, which might lead to the possibility of a treatment that might give me some more time, then I was prepared to make the move.

He said that I must understand that he couldn't make any promises about the outcome, but one thing he was sure of was that there was nothing more that could be done for me here at Hereford. I nodded my understanding of what he was saying and then he left, saying that he would be able to let me know more about the timing of the move in the morning.

After he had gone I texted Helen to put her in the picture. She texted back saying she was pleased at my decision and that she would be sure to see me before I left for Birmingham.

I went to bed with mixed feelings about what the next day might bring but, strangely, a bit happier that at least a decision had been made.

Tuesday 13th December

It wasn't until I put my watch on that I noticed the date. I know for some people that the 13th is associated with bad luck, but being a child born on the 13th I had, at an early age, come to realise that nice things can happen as well: such as having parties and receiving presents, so I was quite relaxed about my move in the hope that it too could lead to some happiness.

Jim arrived about 11.00am; pretty good for a teenager on a day off, I thought, and what's more he had brought some blueberry ice with him, so things were already moving in a positive direction when the consultant arrived. His general disposition added to the buoyant feeling, particularly when he confirmed that this was indeed going to be 'D' day. He said that he had arranged for an ambulance to do the transfer and that it would be available between 2.00 and 2.30pm. However, he emphasised that I would have to go straight away when the ambulance crew arrived and asked me to please make sure that I had everything packed up and ready to go, which I assured him that I would. He finished by saying that, unfortunately, because of his workload at Hereford he could not make it to Birmingham until the next day, but that everything was in place and, finally, he wished me good luck for the journey.

I started by collecting together my wash things, the cards that people had sent and, under my direction, Jim began packing the items and all my clothes into the holdall that Helen had put out for him to bring with him. She had even included some carrier bags for any of the clothes that needed washing. We worked quickly as a team and then checked and checked again to make sure that everything was packed away and, once satisfied that the job was done and Helen wouldn't be able to find anything that we had forgotten, we sat and waited ……. and waited, ……. and waited, it seemed like forever.

I was expecting Helen to be back by about 1.30ish and, getting a bit edgy now that it was nearly ten to two, I asked Jim if he wouldn't mind popping out to the car park to see if she was coming. After twenty minutes or so he returned without having had any success and I couldn't phone Helen to find out where she was because, not having a hands free kit in the car, she always switched her phone off while driving.

I started to panic a bit when the ambulance crew arrived, and asked whether I was ready to go. I said that I was but that my wife had not returned yet and would there be any chance that they could hang on for a short while. They checked their watches and after a short conflab said that they could, but only for a few minutes and said that while they were waiting they might as well take a wander down the corridor to the Nurses' Station.

Now I was really worried that Helen wouldn't make it back in time, so I asked Jim if he would go to the car park again and if he saw Mum to let her know that she needed to hurry. He went off at a fast pace and returned quite quickly this time saying that there was still no sign of her.

All of the day's plans seemed to be unravelling and then, to top it all off, the ambulance crew came back. They said that they were sorry but it was not possible to delay the journey any longer and that we must make a move. No amount of my or Jim's pleading for an extension of time could sway them in any way, and I was asked to get onto the trolley which they had brought with them from the back of the ambulance. I was surprised at having to use the trolley, and asked them why they were using it rather than a wheelchair. They explained that the choice was made in order to avoid having to make a transfer from one to the other at the back of the ambulance out in the cold.

I was dressed in my jumper over a polo shirt with jogger bottoms and sporting a pair of trainers without socks, the NG tube tucked in behind my left ear.

They pulled the trolley into the room from the corridor and asked me if I could manage to get onto it. They then adjusted the pillows behind my shoulders and wrapped me in a string vest type blanket, and then, making sure that I was comfortable, they strapped me down tightly.

Once they were happy that I was secured in place, they lifted the head of the trolley to about half way so that I could see what was going on; they had also allowed me to keep my arms free. I used my right elbow to hold onto the holdall and held a spit bowl with my right hand, just in case the change of air temperature caused me to have a coughing fit and then, finally, they placed a lightweight oxygen canister and mask on the foot of the trolley.

As all this was going on Jim anxiously paced up and down and, at one point, he walked as far as the corner of the main corridor and back to see if Helen was coming but when he got back he shook his head to let me know that there was still no sign of her. On seeing this the ambulance crew apologised again but said that they really couldn't wait any longer. So this small travelling carnival, with Jim following behind carrying the rest of my belongings, wheeled its way to the Nurses' Station one last time and then back along the main corridor to the lifts. Once at ground floor level we detoured via the A&E department, through the exit doors to the ambulance bay, which was situated adjacent to the main public car park.

Just as I was about to be loaded into the back of the ambulance there was a sudden screech of brakes and the sound of ABS bringing a car to a shuddering halt. From my elevated position on the trolley, I could just see around the side of the ambulance to where Helen's silver Suzuki four by four had come to a halt. It was as close as she could get it to the ambulance, but still be within the perimeter of the car park.

The driver's door suddenly burst open; Helen jumped out and ran full tilt towards us with her coat tails flapping. As she ran she yelled for us to wait and Jim asked the ambulance crew if they could hold on because this was my wife. They stopped the trolley and as Helen caught up to the ambulance she asked Jim to go and look after the car which was still stood with its door wide open.

First looking at me and then at the crew, she thanked them for waiting but they said she needed to be quick with her goodbyes as they had to get under way. Helen was close to tears by now at the thought of nearly missing my departure. I held her with my right arm, but she struggled to embrace me across the holdall full of clothes. The ambulance driver said that they couldn't take her in the back of the ambulance with me so she said that she would follow us to Birmingham.

My first thought was for Helen, so I said to her that it would be getting late by the time I was booked in and sorted out at Birmingham and, therefore, it would probably be better if she visited me in the hospital the next day, but she insisted that she had to see me safely settled in, otherwise she would be too worried to sleep. To avoid aggravating the ambulance crew, by causing any further delay, we quickly agreed that she should take Jim home, get something to eat and then use my Volvo saloon to travel the long distance to Birmingham and back, on the understanding that Jim accompanied her on the journey. All agreed I kissed her on the forehead; then she stood back so that they could finally load me into the ambulance and, as the rear doors were being closed, I could see her wave and blow me a kiss.

Once on board and the trolley locked into place, one of the crew made themselves busy attaching me to a blood pressure monitor and making me comfortable on the trolley for the journey, while the other jumped into the cab and started the engine.

We moved at a slow pace out of the car park and into the traffic on the main road leading out of Hereford, and from where I was positioned with the back of the trolley raised I was able to see out of the side window of the ambulance. I could make out retail stores, side roads, pedestrians on the pavements and other vehicles going by and, it slowly dawned on me, that this might be the last time that I would see such things because this could well be the last cognitive road journey I would make.

One of the things we had always liked about Hereford was that it's not a big city and therefore it was not long before the view from the window changed, from a suburban landscape to rolling countryside and with the afternoon sun behind us I could see everything quite clearly. I tried to take it all in for one last time and, as we turned slightly south, over the brow of a hill, I could actually see the sun, big and round just above the horizon, and just for a moment I stared straight at it, unblinkingly, willing its life giving rays to shine in through my eyes and down my optic nerves to burn out this thing growing inside me.

The ambulance crested the hill which made the sun disappear from view. I closed my eyes tightly and could still see two retained images of swirling bright circles in varying shades of green, orange and white, as though they were just hovering in front of me and, not wanting to lose the image, I kept them shut until the mirages dissolved into the backs of my eyelids.

The sun started to set and the light gradually faded, the passing scenery became more like shadows than solid things, and then the lights inside the ambulance were switched on. Suddenly everything outside looked black and in the window all I could see was the reflected mirror image of the interior fittings and the ghostly face of the crew member. With the darkness came the feeling of being shut in, rather than seeing out and so I laid back. The attending crew member asked if I was alright and I nodded. I had already made him aware of my difficulty with speaking and so there was very limited conversation between us.

The journey proceeded at a reasonable pace, the crew chatted to each other and I could occasionally see lights on farm buildings in the distance or headlights of passing vehicles and sometimes we would pass under street lights at a roundabout. Eventually, after an hour or so we reached the motorway. The time was now about 5.00pm and with the traffic on the motorway virtually at a standstill progress slowed to a snail's pace and, since looking out into the darkness had made me feel chilly, I signalled to the crew member who covered me with another blanket.

Now whether it was the dust caused by the unfolding of the blanket or some other reason I don't know, but I started to have a retching coughing fit which brought immediate attentive concern. My mouth felt very dry with my damaged tongue wagging around like a dry stick, however, between coughs, I managed to croak that I needed a drink of water. I was surprised to be told that ambulances do not carry drinking water; the only thing they had on board for me to drink were some small ampoules of sterile eyewash water. I said that anything would do, so he opened a drawer and dug out a small plastic vial and breaking off the snib he handed it to me.

I gently squeezed about half of the water into my mouth, being careful not to swallow any, for fear of aggravating the coughing and then let the water sit as a small puddle in the bottom of my mouth allowing my tongue to wallow in it.

Gradually it seemed to rehydrate and become more pliable as the water slowly dissipated. I didn't use the second half of the water and dropped the vial into the spit bowl on my lap.

The noise of the engine made it difficult for me to understand everything that the crew were saying to each other, but I could tell from their tone that they were disappointed at the lack of progress. However, I did manage to glean from their conversation that they were due to be going to the [works] Christmas party that night but they were saying, because of the heavy traffic, it was very unlikely that they would make it back to Hereford in time.

My feeling of general weakness was starting to make the journey very tiring so I asked the attending crew member how much longer it would be before we reached the hospital. He moved forward and asked the driver who shouted over his shoulder that it would be at least another hour, possibly an hour and a half, with the traffic like this.

In a broken whisper, I said that it was a pity that we couldn't switch the blue lights on to speed our way through the traffic but he replied that they weren't allowed to, not unless I took a turn for the worse. It would need something like my blood pressure to fall, or my not being able to maintain body temperature, or if I suddenly developed chest pains, before that could happen.

Trying to be helpful, I said that I was actually starting to feel quite cold and my throat problem was making me cough a lot more plus, if we got to Birmingham quicker, it might mean that they could get back in time for their Christmas party. He thought for a minute and then stood up and moved forward to speak to the driver and, having considered my suggestion for a short period, they made their decision.

The driver radioed the dispatch centre and said that in their opinion my condition had deteriorated. He said that I was complaining of being cold and having coughing fits, at which point I managed to provide a suitably convincing backing track to his open mike. As we waited, we could hear the dispatcher mumbling to someone else and then, after a short period of consultation off air, a clear voice came back over the speaker giving the driver permission to proceed with 'blues and twos'.

The driver flicked the switch and I could immediately see the flashing blue lights come on, as they reflected off of the side of a large white lorry which was beside us in the next lane. Then, as the two tone horns started to wail, the traffic moved forward slightly, enabling the driver to pull the ambulance into the emergency lane. Within a short distance we had managed to take the slip road off the motorway to a roundabout and speedy progress was restored once more.

A smile flitted across my lips as I lay back onto the pillows. I thought to myself, that after all the hundreds of thousands of miles I had driven in my lifetime, if this was going to be the last journey I would know then, if it couldn't be for pleasure, I could at least get a bit of fun out of it and, although I wouldn't be joining in any Christmas festivities, these guys might be able to get to the 'works' do with their mates. And so it was that after about half an hour we pulled up to the front of the Birmingham hospital.

Directly we stopped the driver fairly leapt from the cab and made his way to the main entrance. I followed his progress from the ambulance window until he was swallowed up by the huge brightly lit glass fronted edifice, which formed the first part of the massive rebuilding project for the whole hospital. I had previously seen news footage of the progress of the hospital regeneration on the TV, but this was the first time that seen it 'in the flesh' so to speak.

The attending crew member asked me if, with his assistance, I would be able to disembark from the ambulance on foot, rather than be wheeled out on the trolley. I confirmed that I was sure that I could and so he took off the top blanket, folded and stowed it away, and then undid the straps that had been holding me for the past couple of hours. This gave me an immediate sense of freedom but, as I tried to stand, I found my legs were like jelly and the crew member had to grab me to stop me from falling. He said that I should lean back against the trolley until some feeling came back to my legs and, as I did so, he draped the remaining blanket over my shoulders while we waited for the driver to return.

Eventually there was a knock on the rear door, which when opened revealed that the driver had returned with a wheelchair. His colleague asked what had taken so long, he shrugged his shoulders and said that there had been some confusion at the admissions desk as they were not expecting my arrival.

This didn't make a lot of sense after what the consultant had told me and I had visions of having to go back to Hereford Hospital, or maybe having to spend the night in one of the many Portakabins around the site, or even that I might be trolley parked in a corridor somewhere until I was found a bed. However, he said that he had managed to convince the admissions co-ordinator that it must have been a communication glitch between the hospital computers and, eventually, they had managed to locate a bed for me.

The ambulance crew assisted me to disembark and sit in the wheelchair. They adjusted the blanket around me, placed my feet onto the foot plates and my belongings onto my lap. While they were doing this I looked around, and in the bright lights of the building I saw other ambulances parked nearby with people coming and going from the hospital which, through its glass façade, I could see had a typically modern interior design.

As we moved off I felt the bitter cold of the winter wind blowing across the open car park on my face, hands and particularly my exposed ankles, so I was quite pleased when the big glass entrance doors hissed open and the warm hospital air enveloped us. We had arrived at the admissions desk and my now rather large medical file was handed over for checking and then returned. At this stage I thought a hospital porter would come to collect me but instead the ambulance crew were given directions as to where they had to take me and we set off through the hospital towards our destination.

At first I was encouraged by the modern facilities but the further we moved away from the entrance area the more we passed through partially refurbished parts of the old building, until eventually we entered an enclosed timber walkway, which I imagined connected the old to the new. Once on the other side we came to a set of double doors. However, instead of heading through them we took a downwards ramp to the right hand side of the doors and descended into a very old part of the basement of the original building.

We turned a corner and faced into a high ceilinged corridor; on the right hand side it had windows with high sills, well they seemed high from my position in the wheelchair and on the left hand side there was a small Nurses' Station adjacent to which was a disabled toilet. Further along the corridor there were two, possibly three, large openings and the corridor beyond that was closed off by a part glazed door. The whole area was brightly illuminated from the ceiling with fluorescent lighting giving it a shadowless hard look. The overall impression was that it was unloved and tatty ….. and it smelled of toilets.

We stopped at the Nurses' Station and my file was once again handed over. The nurse asked me if I was able to walk, which I affirmed that I could and so I, along with my belongings, were offloaded from the wheelchair. The ambulance crew offered their best wishes and, after agreeing with the nurse to return the wheelchair to the entrance area, they walked quickly away, no doubt with the thought of mince pies and several libations uppermost in their minds but with them gone, I felt that I had lost my last contact with the warm, friendly atmosphere of Hereford Hospital and was going to have to face this new alien environment on my own.

Having travelled for more than two hours, my most urgent need was to use the loo so I asked which one to use and the nurse directed me towards the disabled toilet. On entry I found that it was a typically oversized cubicle which had a WC pan centrally along the back wall with all the appropriate adjacent grab rails and a sink, mirror and hand dryer set low on the side wall for the benefit of anyone who had to use a wheelchair. It was all in relatively good nick and so I felt that my first, rather disenchanted, impressions of where I was to spend the next couple of weeks may have been misplaced.

I returned to the Nurses' Station and she escorted me to my bed and, as we rounded the corner of the first opening, I was immediately aware of the level of noise and quickly realised that it was still visiting time and those patients with visitors were chatting, while those who were without all seemed to be talking on their mobile phones.

I could see four beds on either side of the room, each one had a high level rail, below which hung a curtain that finished about two feet off of the floor. As well as the usual medical paraphernalia and gas pipes, the rear wall of each bed space had an angle poise type lamp fixed to it alongside a cantilevered TV screen, which looked as though it might operate much as the one had done at Hereford. I was led to the furthest bed on the right hand side; the nurse placed my holdall on the over bed table and said that I should pull the curtain, get changed into my nightwear and, in the meantime, she would go to fetch me a jug of water. As she walked away I croaked in my poor voice that I couldn't drink water but I don't think that she heard me.

This end of the room had three windows, again all with high sills, and it dawned on me that this was because the floor of the ward was below ground level. Each of the windows had its own roller blind, the one on the furthest window had been pulled down to the sill level, the one in the middle was obviously faulty and hung at a jaunty angle and the one adjacent to my bed had no stop on it, allowing it to hang well below the level of the sill, and partially resting on a large cast iron radiator, which was fitted to the wall between the two bed ends: a few bits and pieces, such as face cloths, had been placed on the top of it to dry.

I nodded hello to the two occupants of the closest beds, and with my right hand gave a cross throat sign while opening and closing my mouth, they seemed to understand that I could not speak properly.

I pulled the curtain closed and, having unpacked the contents of my holdall into the bedside cabinet and placed my nightwear on the over bed table, I sat on the bed, slumped forward and wept. This was how I had imagined things might be and this was the very last place I wanted to spend the rest of my life. Just then the curtain fluttered and I could just see the nurse from the corner of my eye as she came in with the jug of water. I was right, she hadn't heard me say that I couldn't drink anything. On seeing that I was upset she asked if there was anything she could do, but without lifting my head, I shook it slowly and she said, sympathetically, that she would give me a few minutes.

I managed to regain some composure and, with one hand, battled to take off my trainers and disrobe, I then put on a clean 'T' shirt and pyjama trouser bottoms and got onto the bed. The nurse returned, but before entering the curtained enclosure she asked if I was respectable. I tried to make my voice heard but it was inaudible above the general clamour and so a seemingly disembodied, be-capped face appeared through the join in the curtains. It curiously reminded me of a Punch and Judy show, and the humour of it lifted my mood slightly.

Having seen that I had got changed the nurse pulled back the curtain and came to the bedside with a clipboard in her hand. She said that she needed to ask me a few questions for the hospital admissions procedure; however, she said the most important thing was for me to have a hospital wrist band. With that she pulled a length of white plastic from her apron pocket and wrote my details on it, along with my date of birth, and then sealed over the writing with a clear adhesive cover. She then took hold of my left wrist to secure the new band. It was the first time she had noticed the other two wrist bands I was already sporting: a pale green one and the red one signifying my newly acquired allergy to penicillin.

Picking up the clipboard, she said that she must make a note of that on my admission form and then proceeded to ask me a long list of questions about my age, address, next of kin's phone number and whether I been tested for AIDS etc. I let her know that my voice was poor and that she would have to listen closely for my answers. Once she had finished ticking the boxes and scribbling notes she went through the form again in her mind to make sure that she hadn't forgotten anything; then satisfied that all was in place she went to leave. I made a stifled noise to attract her attention, which she must have heard because she turned and, on coming back to the bedside, I asked her about my NG food and medication. She said that, unfortunately, due to my unexpected late arrival nothing had been written up for me and that things could not be sorted until the morning.

Helen and Jim arrived during this conversation and they were just as disconcerted as I was about me not receiving any medication to help control the mucus and assist my sleep. The nurse apologised again, but said that her hands were tied until the doctor had visited the next day.

Having resigned ourselves that nothing could be done to resolve the situation that night Helen was obviously still irritated. She explained, exasperatedly, that having driven the long distance to see me the nurses at the desk would only allow them an extra quarter of an hour past the usual finishing time, which meant they would have to leave again in about half an hour. This was proving very stressful for both of us because at Hereford there had been virtually no restriction on the visiting times owing to my terminal condition but that seemed to hold little sway here. I said to her that I was starting to think that I would have to change my ambivalence to the number thirteen.

Helen raised her eyes and smiled as it dawned on her that today was the thirteenth and after giving a little shrug of her shoulders she then proceeded to unpack and stow some clean clothes and toiletries into the bedside locker. Jim sat on the bed and asked me what the hospital was like but I said that I hadn't really had the time to explore it as yet so I would have to let him know more the next day.

All too soon the visiting bell sounded and, although we stretched it out as long as we could, in the end we had to say our goodbyes. Helen said she would text me to let me know that she had got home safely and again in the morning to see what the consultant had to say. We then waved to each other as Helen and Jim passed from view around the corner by the Nurses' Station.

By now the other patients were in various stages of settling down for the night, some were reading and others had their earphones on while watching the TV so I thought I would do the same for a while to see what was happening about the Buncefield oil fire. I rifled around in my holdall to retrieve my TV card, only to find that this hospital's pay as you go system had been installed by a different provider and that my half used card, which I had brought with me from Hereford did not work. I could see that it was going to be a long night.

The nurse came and pulled back the curtain, as they do at night, and once the ward was settled one of the nurses turned off the main high level lighting, so I dimmed my over bed light and waited for Helen's text which I knew would take some time in coming because of how far it was for her and Jim to get home. I don't know how long it was, but I came to with my mobile phone pinging on the pillow next to me.

Wednesday 14th December

My previous two weeks, secreted in a private ensuite room at Hereford hospital, with the 'early' nurse coming in to open the curtains, check my blood pressure, take my temperature and disconnect my NG tube had, in no way, prepared me for the brutally different start to this day. One minute the ward was all subdued lighting and peaceful and then, just as if someone had fired a starting pistol, it erupted into a cacophony of light and noise with people getting out of bed, nurses coming around to check whether we had survived the night, and patients calling out good morning to each other with one or two even managing to send items crashing to the floor as they collected their toiletries in the rush to be first to the washroom, which prompted memories of my time as an apprentice soldier at Arborfield, back in the 1960's.

During the night I had needed to go to the loo on a couple of occasions, so I had used the disabled toilet, mainly because no-one had shown me where the men's toilets were. It was clean and well-appointed so I thought that maybe my misgivings about this old Victorian pile might be misplaced and that things wouldn't be so bad after all, but I was soon to discover that this was false optimism.

Using my right hand, I rolled my shaving kit, soap and flannel into my towel and headed in the general direction that the other patients had gone. I detoured past the disabled toilet and through a dark blue door in the opposite wall. It was quite a small room with a much lower ceiling than the main ward. Each of the WC and shower cubicles was in use and, as I stood there taking in my surroundings, I noted that the coolness of the room was causing it to fill with steam from the hot showers. Unfortunately the one wall mounted ventilation fan, with no internal cover and a damaged fan blade clacking against the casing, was not coping with it and all the surfaces were covered with a sheen of condensation.

As it was a winter's morning there wasn't much light coming through the high level slit windows on the outside wall and only one of the circular light fittings was working, making the room very gloomy. Through the big burn hole in the cover of the broken light fitting, I could see that they were the cheap commercial type with a black plastic base, a translucent plastic cover and an upturned foil pie case above the lamp, acting as a reflector. The ceiling was painted gloss white and the walls were a mid-blue; well, that is those areas that weren't covered with a layer of black mildew and the floor surface consisted of dark red quarry tiles. It was quite obvious that the general maintenance of these old Victorian buildings had been put on a back burner during the regeneration programme.

The steamy atmosphere was starting to make me cough so, thinking that I might use the disabled loo instead, I turned and left. However, I found that someone else had already had that bright idea and so I shuffled out into the main corridor to find the nearest public toilets where, because it was outside visiting hours, I was able to carry out my ablutions almost uninterrupted. I came to the conclusion that in future, much like when Helen and I went camping, I would delay using the showers until the afternoons.

As I made my way back to my bed, I could see from the corridor that the blinds in the room had been opened. However, I was baffled as to why I couldn't see any daylight but then, as I got closer, I realised just how far below ground level we were and on reaching my own bed, I found that I had to look up through the window at a fairly steep angle before I could see the sky.

I was busily rearranging my locker contents, following its rushed stowage of the previous evening, and didn't notice the consultant arrive at my bed so I was surprised to see him standing there when I turned round, particularly so at this early hour. He said that he would be back to do his normal rounds later, but that afternoon he would be going to a meeting to push for me to have a PET scan. However, he felt that he needed a bargaining chip to help him make a strong case. He suggested that it might go in my favour if I agreed to have a live biopsy taken of the cancerous growth.

He said this could possibly be to my own advantage and would also assist future research better than a post mortem sample; plus he could argue at the meeting that my cooperation would be to the benefit of others. Not sure what a live biopsy would entail, I asked him to explain the procedure. He said that under anaesthetic an incision would be made in my neck just behind my left ear and a small amount of tissue would be gathered from the growth. I asked him if there would there be any side effects. He paused for a minute and then said that some damage to the nerves in my neck couldn't be ruled out altogether. However, he thought this would be unlikely and from the point of the view of arguing my case the benefits would outweigh the risks. I thought that having made the decision to come to Birmingham to have a PET scan in the first place, this additional intervention would not amount to much, so I told him that I would agree to have the biopsy. His smile told me he thought that he would now be able to achieve a positive outcome.

About 11.00am the consultant, accompanied by a retinue of about eight junior doctors, re-entered the ward on their normal rounds. I realised that I must have been his only patient on this ward because they came straight to my bedside and, as they clustered around the foot of the bed, the last one in the line pulled the curtain closed behind them.

The consultant asked me if I had any objection to his team being there. I shook my head and he then introduced me to his 'mini-mes' who, almost in unison, chorused a cheery greeting from which I could tell that, unlike me, they were quite excited to be there. The consultant reached for my file in the rack at the end of the bed and, having checked my obs record, he proceeded to explain to his team the unusual nature of my condition. As he read the notes and gesticulated his explanation, it was difficult to avoid the eight pairs of eyes staring at me which seemed to open wider or become more intense the longer the oration continued. He concluded, rather matter-of-factly I thought, by saying that intervention was not an option in my case but that I been brought to Birmingham for a confirmation PET scan and had agreed to having a live biopsy done to assist with research. I thought for a minute that the 'mini-mes' were going to break into spontaneous applause.

In my broken whisper, I then asked the consultant what was happening about my NG food, because I hadn't received any nutrition since before I left Hereford. He seemed somewhat nonplussed to be asked a question regarding an obvious oversight on his behalf, particularly now that he had become the focus of eight pairs of enquiring eyes. The consultant sort of stammered, seemingly thrown by this omission, but then collecting his thoughts together he said in a firm voice, obviously trying to regain his standing in front of the junior doctors, that he would arrange for the dietician to come and sort out my requirements as a matter of urgency and then, seemingly to further demonstrate his competence, he said that he would also write up my medication to avoid any further delay.

While he made notes, I reminded him about my atropine patches again; slightly wrong footed by another of my questions he frowned, and said that he didn't think the hospital used them anymore but, as if to offload the question, he turned to his team and put it to them that if atropine patches were not available what else could be used. There was a brief huddle, and then one of the young women doctors suggested that, because some eye drops contained atropine, maybe they could be prescribed instead.

The 'mini-mes' all nodded approval of this suggestion and the consultant said that he would arrange for a bottle of eye drops to be sent from the pharmacy. He said that I could self-administer them by placing a couple of drops under my tongue as required, although I should use it sparingly and so, with their business concluded, the consultant said that he would keep me informed of the outcome of the meeting and then, bidding me goodbye, he wheeled his team out through the curtains.

I was sat there, mulling over what had just occurred when my mobile phone went 'Ping!'; it was Helen texting me to let me know that she was about to leave home and asking me if there was anything that I needed. I texted back saying that there was nothing I could think of, to which she reply texted, 'OK see you soon'.

Helen arrived with Jim around 3.00pm, I explained what had happened to me so far and both raised their eyebrows when I mentioned having to put eye drops in my mouth but then, much to my delight, Helen produced the now customary small vacuum flask of broken, flavoured ice cubes.

Jim asked me whether I had seen the latest news about the oil fire but I told him that I couldn't, because my TV card was the wrong type for these televisions so Helen gave him some cash and asked him if he would go and see if he could locate a dispensing machine.

While Jim was off on his quest, a middle aged woman came to the bed and introduced herself as the dietician.

She was carrying a clip board like a tray using both hands and it had a yoghurt pot balanced on top. She said that she had been asked to assess me for being able to eat solids and thickened liquids. I explained in a whisper that I had only been able to have NG food for the past two weeks and, although I could manage to swallow some flavoured ice, I was not able to drink fluids at all.

She sat on the edge of the bed and asked me some general questions which I answered, enabling her to tick them off on her list. She then said that she would like see me try some flavoured mousse. At this point she removed the foil top and dipped the spoon into its contents, and handed me the pot from which I dutifully removed a spoonful of mousse. However, because my tongue was damaged and not working properly I had to put the spoon well into my mouth to enable me to close my lips. As my mouth shut, the mousse squidged off of the spoon and into my throat, causing me to have a massive reflux coughing fit and, because my lips refused to release the spoon, the mousse was forced out of my nostrils.

Through my half opened, tear filled eyes, I could see the dietician physically jump backwards and Helen squirm with embarrassment at the sight. I grabbed the box of tissues from the over bed table and, just in time, I managed with my one good hand to remove the spoon and catch the remainder of the mousse, as a sneeze burst out of my mouth.

With Helen's assistance we cleaned the offending residue from my face and hands. I smiled at the dietician and asked rhetorically, hadn't it gone well. Helen, after her initial distaste, found that now she could hardly stop herself from laughing out loud, and the dietician conceded that it would probably be best for me to continue with the NG food for the time being. However, she said that if I could swallow broken ice then I might be able to swallow some thickened liquid and set off to make me a cup of tea.

In the meantime, Jim, having managed to find a TV card dispenser, came back and proceeded to make sure that the new card operated the television. As the picture emerged out of the blank screen I thanked him and then Helen and I told him of the preceding mousse swallowing kerfuffle, which he found totally amusing so much so that, when the dietician arrived back with the cup of tea, he made sure that he took up a position which would give him an unobstructed view.

The dietician returned with a paper cup full of tea and I could see from the colour it was very milky. She assured me that it was not hot and proceeded to stir in something that resembled granulated sugar and, as she stirred, I could see the tea noticeably thicken, becoming the consistency of runny custard. Satisfied with the condition of the contents, she handed the cup to me but, before I imbibed, I made sure that I had tissues at the ready then, tipping the cup towards my lips, I took the smallest of sips. The taste was absolutely disgusting. I didn't know how I managed keep myself from retching unless it was just so that Jim would have nothing to laugh at.

I dribbled the small amount of tea back into the cup and then took another small sip and, this time, I did actually manage a swallow but, having achieved the goal and not wishing to prolong the torment further, I waved the cup away. The dietician said that with practice I might be able to improve my swallow and therefore she would leave some thickener for me to use if I wanted to. She also said that she would arrange for a pump and NG food supply to be provided. Thankfully, after she had gone, I found that there were still some pieces of ice left in the flask which I eagerly swallowed to try and take away the awful flavour of the thickened tea.

As the afternoon morphed into early evening, the three of us reflected on how we had managed to find humour in the midst of our heartbreak and then, all too soon, it came time for Helen and Jim to make tracks.

One of the major differences between Hereford and Birmingham hospitals, no doubt simply because of the size of the place, was that nothing happened quickly; so Helen and Jim must have been well on their way home before a nurse brought the pump and NG food; coincidentally, almost at the same time as a small white box containing the bottle of eye drops arrived from the pharmacy.

The nurse said that because of the delay she had better get me onto the food straight away. However, as I didn't intent to settle down just yet, I was still in my 'T' shirt and joggers with my dressing gown on over the top, so I lay on the bed while the nurse set up the equipment. Having manged to fit all of the separate parts together, she finally connected me to the NG tube and switched on the pump, checking that all was working before she left to continue with her duties elsewhere.

I reached up and pulled the TV round and flicked through the channels but, on finding that there were no news channels running at the time, I chose a history channel instead and watched someone build and test a trebuchet. After I had been watching for a while, I started to feel dampness around my neck and left shoulder, I reached over with my right hand only to discover that the NG tube had become disconnected and had oozed its contents onto my pillow and down into the bed. In panic mode I quickly managed to pull myself up and swing my legs over the edge of the bed and, dragging the stand towards me, I switched off the pump. Surveying the mess I quickly realized that it was more of a problem than could be coped with using a few tissues, so I pushed the emergency button on the bed console. A nurse appeared at the end of the ward and looked towards my bed as much as to say, "Do you really need me?"

I signalled the problem to her by waving the loose end of the NG tube, and pointing to the now rather large brown stain on the shoulder of my otherwise white towelling robe. On arriving at the bed side she could see that my request had not been uncalled for so, in a caring tone, she told me not to worry and that it would soon be cleared up. As I had not showered yet that day I suggested to her that now might be a good time, while the bed was being changed, to which she agreed. So, taking my towel, toilet bag and a clean shirt, I made my way to the washroom, where I was pleased to find that I was on my own with all the facilities available. However, with the light still broken and the wall fan continuing to play its sad lament, even the lack of steam couldn't improve my initial impression from first thing this morning.

I entered one of the shower cubicles, but because of the mildew everywhere I couldn't find a surface where I wanted to put my belongings down and, to make things worse, there was a hole in the back of the door where the coat hook should have been. However, 'Needs must when the devil drives,' they say, so balancing the toiletries precariously, one on top of the other on the high window sill, I dug around in the depths of my toilet bag and found a small pair of nail clippers, and pushed their narrow end firmly into the hole in the door so that I could use it as a clothes peg and then, using a combination of moves which were something between playing chess and Twister, I at last managed to have a shower.

Luckily, by the time I got back to the ward the bed had already been dealt with, so I stowed my soiled clothes into one of the bin bags Helen had left and then reconnected my NG tube, but this time I gave the connection a robust tug before switching on the pump, which then whirred into life causing the beige liquid from the bag slowly to fill the tube; all seemed well.

The efforts of the day and the warm shower had made me feel tired, so carefully circumnavigating the food pump stand, making sure not to twist the NG tube on the way, I got into bed to wait for my medication to arrive. Once settled, I sent a text to Helen asking her please to bring in some clean clothes and my other dressing gown. She texted back, asking what had happened. I replied nothing serious and that I would tell her the whole sorry story the next day.

I watched as the drugs trolley nurse did her rounds; she had a full figure' as my mum would have said and, when she arrived at my bed I could see that she was a real 'copper knob', with bright sparkly green eyes and a warm smile. She was wearing a white apron over a striped dress and had a white nurse's cap pinned to her hair. She first checked my chart and next my wrist bands; she then asked me my date of birth and, once the formalities were over and satisfied as to my identity, she tipped some tablets into a small wax paper cup and reached for the water jug and glass. I was quite alarmed to think that she was expecting me to swallow the tablets, so I held my hand out in a 'stop' gesture. She looked puzzled, so I explained about the problems with my throat, and she said I shouldn't worry, she would be back later after she had completed the last couple of patients.

I assumed that she would go to get some different medication and, sure enough, when the nurse reached the end of the ward she disappeared from view, only to reappear shortly afterwards carrying a mortar and pestle with a large needleless syringe half filled with a clear liquid. Now it was my turn to look puzzled as she placed the mortar and pestle on the over bed table, giving me the weirdest feeling that I had been transported back to

Dickensian times, particularly within these Victorian surroundings.

The nurse tipped the tablets from the small cup into the mortar and picking up the pestle she worked them into a find powder, she then emptied the contents of the syringe into the mortar. Seeing my look of concern, she smiled and said I shouldn't worry as she hadn't just got it out of a tap, it was saline solution. She then proceeded to stir it into the powder and, once satisfied that the powder had completely dissolved, she refilled the syringe and fitted the needleless end into the cannula on the back of my hand, and slowly depressed the plunger.

It contained quite a lot more fluid than I usually received, which stung and made me flinch. She asked me if I was OK, I grimaced a bit but nodded anyway. When the syringe had been emptied she asked me when was the last time that I had the cannula changed. I said that I hadn't, it was the same one the junior doctor had inserted when I first arrived at Hereford hospital. She gave me that one raised eyebrow look which suggested that this was not a normal situation. Having finished giving me the prescribed drugs she locked the drugs cabinet, leaving it at the foot of the bed and said that she would be back in a minute.

A short time later she returned carrying a kidney dish with a small bottle of liquid, some cotton wool balls and another cannula in a cellophane wrapper. She gently tried to remove the sticking plaster which held the old cannula in place but, as she struggled with the hardened adhesive, the cannula and a piece of flesh about 12mm diameter and 3mm thick, just came away, but to my surprise it didn't hurt or bleed. I just stared at this gaping hole in the back of my hand. The nurse, seeing my alarm at the sight, said that it should have been changed some time ago but, because it hadn't, the flesh around it had necrotised and that was why the wound hadn't bled. She then opened the bottle and put some liquid onto a cotton wool ball and dabbed at the wound; I expected it to sting but again there was no pain. She then placed a clean cotton wool ball in the wound and secured it with a cross of sticking plaster and told me to try not to get it wet and that she would keep an eye on it over the next couple of days. In the meantime she said that I would need another cannula put in straight away, in case I needed further drug intervention. However, she said that it wouldn't be a good idea to put it into my good right arm, because this would restrict my movement if I had to have a drip of some kind, so she decided to insert it into the inside left forearm. Having secured the cannula with a strip of sticking plaster, she cleared away the debris, placed the kidney dish and the mortar and pestle on top of the drugs trolley, smiled, said goodnight and left.

After such a long and tiring day I just wanted to go to sleep, but thought that before retiring I had better take some eye drops to keep my throat clear. There is a certain reticence you have to overcome, when the label on the box states in bold block capital letters **EXTERNAL USE ONLY** and you have been told to put some in your mouth. However, trusting in the competence of the consultant, I put two drops from the dropper under my tongue as instructed. The result was immediate and felt like what I can only describe as like sucking on half a dozen lemons but without the taste. My mouth felt completely dried out in an instant, and I could feel my cheeks concaving against my teeth.

Exhausted, I laid back on the bed wondering if I would ever see the dawn and fell asleep.

Thursday 15ᵗʰ December

My day crashed open again with all the noise and hubbub of a large busy hospital; my first waking thought was that my being able to see the ceiling must mean that I hadn't died in the night, a thought emphasised by the tea lady as she rattled through with the breakfast trolley and the sound of nurses busily taking the first round of 'obs' for the day.

One of the nurses came over and raised the window blinds and I could see from the fog swirling into the area outside the window from the ground level above that it must be a cold morning; then looking to my left I saw that my food bag was empty, so I pulled the stand towards me, switched off the pump and disconnected the NG tube ……….freedom! However, it didn't take long for me to realise that the re-sited cannula was going to be a problem, because every time I tried to move my arm it would catch on one thing or another, like the bed cover or my clothes and, each time, it hurt.

Anyway, free of the food pump, I checked my phone for any texts from family and friends letting me know that they were thinking of me and as usual there were several. This had now become my usual practice both first thing in the morning and last thing at night. Once I had answered the texts, I headed for the wash room and managed to get through my basic ablutions without too much hassle but this was mostly because I didn't attempt to have a shower.

They were making the bed when I got back to the ward. So I was sitting in the chair waiting for them to finish when a junior doctor, wearing the obligatory white coat and carrying a stethoscope, came and informed me that I had been booked in for a CAT scan, either later on in the morning or early in the afternoon, as soon as a slot became available. I thanked him for the information and thought that at least it would give some interest to the day. By now the bed was made so while I waited for a porter to come, I got on top of the covers to watch the TV, in an effort to get an update on the oil fire and, after searching through the channels, I managed to find out that it had reignited the night before and the fire authorities had made the decision to let it burn itself out, which with my safety advisor hat on I thought was probably the safest thing they could do.

Around midday a porter finally arrived with a wheelchair; he took me through a labyrinth of corridors and, I don't know why, but for some reason being in this hospital made me feel like an extra, taking part in the filming of 'Casualty' or 'Holby City'. We rounded a corner and arrived at the X-Ray/Radiology Department. I was certainly glad that I had been escorted, because I would never have found my way there and back on my own.

I was deposited in a large waiting room where there was a receptionist sat at a desk. I could see that there was another patient in a wheelchair and several other people sat waiting in their normal daytime clothes, wearing coats, hats and anoraks. I could see that this was going to take some time and the blanket that the porter had placed in the chair before I sat in it proved to be very handy as I wrapped it around me to keep the draught out.

CAT scan completed, the porter came and took me back to the ward and, a short time later, Kate and Helen arrived. They were keen for me to tell them about the events that happened after visiting time the night before, so I related the story of the disconnected food tube, which prompted Helen to get out a black bin liner and fill it with all the dirty clothes.

I said to them that I had seen on the TV that the oil fire had reignited and that it was lucky that there had not been any rain, the latter statement bringing puzzled expressions from both of them, so I explained that the relatively good weather had allowed the smoke to be blown out sea whereas, if it had rained heavily, the soot and chemicals would have been washed out of the smoke, causing significant pollution of the land. Helen said she was pleased that I had found something to spark my interest and take my mind off things.

Sometime into the afternoon Kate said she needed to talk to me about something. I asked her if she meant on my own, but she replied that it wouldn't be necessary because mum already knew about it. She pulled the curtain part way round the bed and in sombre tone started to explain that she had a very difficult decision to make, but didn't know how to tell me about it, to which Helen confirmed that Kate had been very upset.

It transpired that the problem revolved around flights back to New Zealand. Kate had been on the internet and discovered that, unless she caught the flight due out on that coming Sunday, it would be into the New Year before she could get home to see the children, because all of the flights were booked up with people travelling for the Christmas holidays.

She grabbed some of the tissues to wipe her eyes and blow her nose, then with a tearful voice she continued that emotionally she was being absolutely torn apart because, on one side she wanted to stay to help mum through to the end but, on the other, she knew that after more than two weeks away, Gary and the two girls were missing her dreadfully and desperately hoping that she would be at home for Christmas. I knew that I had to put her mind at rest, so I held her hand and told her there was nothing for her to be upset about. I said that she had shown her love for mum and me by coming from the other side of the world to be with us at this terrible time and we had known from the start that she couldn't stay with us indefinitely. I finished by saying that it was more important for her to be with her own family at this time of year.

The three of us huddled together; Kate's sobbing slowly began to subside now that she had excised the problem which had evidently haunted her over the past couple of days and, as we sat back I told her with as much firmness I could muster, out of my own emotional melt down that, later on, I didn't want her to spend any more of their hard earned money buying a flight back for my funeral because she had been with us when it counted, while I was still alive, and supported mum by helping out at the house at the weekends when it was full of visitors. In an emotional voice Kate thanked me and put her arm around my shoulder.

The afternoon tea trolley arrived and Kate managed to cadge a cup each for both her and Helen and this helped to mollify the upset.

Much later, after visiting had finished, I was laid on the bed engrossed in a history programme on the TV with my earphones on and so I didn't see the consultant enter the ward. In fact it wasn't until he was virtually at my bedside that I became aware of his presence. I was a bit taken aback to see him, because I knew that this was his normal day to be at Hereford Hospital and from his demeanour I could tell he wasn't at all comfortable being here.

Firstly, he said that he was able to confirm that the PET scan had been approved, and it had been booked in for the following afternoon at 2.30pm. I thought, "Well that's the good news, what's the bad?" and waited for him to continue. He confirmed that he had, in fact, made a special trip to see me that evening because he had been contacted by the radiographer regarding the outcome of my CAT scan and, because he knew it was my wish to be kept fully informed of the facts surrounding my case, he felt bound to come and let me know, as soon as he was able, that unfortunately the news was not good.

I knew it! I braced myself for the worst. He said that the result of the scan seemed to show that the cancer had begun to spread and that there was the distinct possibility that metastases had started to form around the area of my left ear.

I threw my head back on the pillow and closed my eyes tightly as the heat of rage engulfed me. I found it so difficult to comprehend that all of this was supposed to be going on inside of me and yet I could feel no pain or discomfort. The moment passed and I opened my eyes again. I looked at the consultant and asked him what was going to happen next. The consultant leaned against the wall, seemingly a bit more relaxed now that he had imparted the news. He said that he didn't want to make a further assessment until after he could see in more detail from the results of the PET scan the next day how the cancer was spreading.

I thanked him for making the special trip, although inside me I knew it was a hollow accolade because I had certainly not wanted to hear the news that he had brought with him, and although it had me very anxious, I decided that I would not let Helen know the news until the morning to save her further distress.

Despite the diazepam I had a very disturbed night.

Friday 16th December

Because of the disturbed night, I had been awake for some time waiting for the day to start, so I decided to get up and make my way to the wash room, hoping to beat the rush of my bedfellows and be ready for my big day. Unfortunately I didn't quite manage this, because as I entered the still dimly lit room, I could hear the dulcet tones of another patient crooning away, accompanied by the almost melodic splashing of the shower water hitting the cubicle floor and the steady rim shot drum beat of the faulty fan.

As I moved further into the room I could see that the cool air was already full of steam. Undeterred, I found the only wash basin with a plug and, using just my right arm, I was able to alternately wipe the mirror and shave myself, all the while trying to take as little time as possible, lest the room should become inundated and all the shower cubicles taken.

Luckily no-one else arrived, so I moved to the shower cubicle which I had previously used and, after I had managed to re-implant my "clothes hook" nail clippers into the hole in the back of the door, I successfully managed one-handedly to disrobe, shower and dry myself without too much hassle. However getting dressed again with one hand and wet feet was a bit of a 'faff'; sometimes underpants can be a garment too far.

Having made this early start meant that there would be a long wait until I was due to be taken for the PET scan and it was still much too early to burden Helen with the news from last night, so I draped my wet towel over the radiator to dry, and straightened out the bedcovers as best I could so that I could get onto the bed to watch the TV. The early morning news confirmed that the Buncefield oil fire had burned itself out and I contented myself that, if nothing else at least, my prediction that it would be extinguished before me had come true.

About 10.00am, I summoned whatever reserves of emotional strength I had left; I texted Helen to tell her the news which the consultant had imparted the previous evening. She immediately phoned back and both of us, fighting back the tears, spent some time trying to console each other but there was little comfort to be had at the end of a phone.

A nurse came and told me that I should make sure that I was wearing something loose and comfortable for the PET scan, because it might take some time. I told her that I had struggled with fits of coughing during the previous scans; she said that she would go and see if anything could be done to alleviate the problem, but said that it might help if I used some of the eye drops to dry up my throat just before I left the ward.

The porter duly arrived with a wheelchair at the appointed time. I had hoped that I would get to see Helen before I was wheeled away, but it was not to be so I quickly texted to her that I was on my way down for the PET scan. Just as we were about to leave, another nurse came to the bedside carrying a large hand held contraption. She explained that it was a suction device for clearing saliva from my throat and that she would be accompanying me to the radiology department. I said wryly, that I wondered how the cleaners would manage without one of their vacuums; she winked at me and said that she had wiped the hose and emptied the bag before bringing it.

We arrived at a room with a small reception area, the porter deposited my notes with the receptionist and then left calling in on his walkie-talkie that his task was completed. The nurse said she would wait with me until I was called through for the radioactive injection and then she would see me again in the scanner room.

My turn came, and a lady wheeled me into a small room with an examination couch which was covered in a length of disposable blue paper and adjacent there was a stainless steel bench with sliding cupboard doors underneath. She explained the procedure to me in some detail, telling me that once I had been given the injection of the radioactive isotope I would have to lay quietly for about half an hour for it to work its way around my body, and that, while this was happening, I might get a feeling of being hot all over but that I shouldn't be concerned, because this was a normal reaction of the body. She continued that a further reaction would be that my urine would become brilliant yellow and that I would remain radioactive for a period of twenty four hours, which meant that I must not come into contact with any pregnant women and that if, accidentally, I was to lose control of my bodily functions during this period then I must let those who were sent to clean it up know that I was radioactive.

Apprehension caused by this information made my thoughts scuttle about all over the place. However, I seem to remember that she then left the room, returning a short while later wearing, what I can only call a body armour tabard and carrying a box with a radioactive sign on the outside and, I can't remember exactly, but she might also have been wearing protective goggles as well. She asked me to lie on the couch, which I did and she then opened the box and produced a large syringe; I was a little disappointed that it wasn't humming or glowing.

After the contents of the syringe had been emptied into me, she clipped a yellow band to my wrist, which signified that I was now radioactive. She then said that she would leave me for a short time while the isotope got to work and, as she left the room, she dimmed the lights. Sure enough as I lay there in the half-light, I could feel the heat start flooding into me; it felt like I was lying in a bath of very hot water but being heated from the inside out. I can only imagine that it's a feeling akin to what ladies suffer during menopausal hot flushes.

The required time passed and the hot flush seemed to be dissipating a bit. I was taken by wheelchair to the scanner room. The PET scanner was definitely the 'big boy' of the scanner family which I had come to know and love over the past few weeks. The large white doughnut seemed to fill the room, and a green glass viewing panel was set in the wall opposite the foot of the sliding table. One of the radiographers and the nurse who had accompanied me from the ward, who had now also adorned herself in a protective tabard, assisted me to get onto the table.

My head was held in between two padded blocks, and a wedge shaped cushion was placed under my knees. A disembodied voice boomed over the speaker asking me if I was comfortable, because the scan would take some time to complete, during which I must keep as still as possible. The voice continued saying that they were aware of the problem with my throat and that if, at any time, I required assistance I should raise my hand to give a signal and the nurse would come to see what was wrong. Then all systems go, the radiographer left the room, leaving me in the care of a rather concerned looking nurse.

The scanner started up and noisily droned on and on, as the table slowly fed me head first into the central hole; it was taking much longer than any of the previous scans I had undergone. It wasn't long before I could feel saliva building up in my mouth and so, as instructed, I raised my hand and the nurse carried the suction device to the table. I said that I thought that I was going to choke and managed to part turn my head to the left towards her, as far as the restriction of the blocks would allow, so that she could insert the suction tube into my mouth. Holding the tube in her left hand she then reached down with her right to switch the suction machine on.

Nothing happened!

She tried again, but the machine still failed to start. The disembodied voice enquired if there was a problem. The nurse, who looked slightly embarrassed, said to me that she would go and have a word with the radiographer. As she left the room I started to panic a bit, I could feel the pool of saliva moving towards the back of my mouth and I knew that a coughing fit would ensue. The disembodied voice boomed again; it said that the pass was nearly complete and that, if possible, I should stay as still as I could for a few more minutes and so, with the help of little rasping coughs, I managed to keep my throat clear until the pass was complete.

The table returned to the starting position, and I felt relieved that it was over because the previous hot flush had now been replaced by a definite chilliness. Then, as soon as my head cleared the machine I half sat up and, just in time, the nurse arrived with a spit bowl. Having managed to clear my throat, the nurse said that I should wait where I was until the radiographers gave the all clear. However, much to my angst, rather than say all was complete and I could go, the voice from behind the screen said that, while the isotope was still radioactive, they wanted to do another pass but that they would give me a ten minute break so that I could get up and walk around for a bit if I wanted to but the voice said that I was not allowed to go to the toilet. The nurse called out to the radiographers that her shift was coming to an end so she would have to leave soon. The voice came back saying that it would be fine but would she please make sure to take her useless piece of equipment with her!

The whole procedure was repeated, during which time I managed to stop from coughing by tilting my head to the left but, I could see from the clock on the wall, that it was now getting on towards 6.30pm and I had been away from the ward for nearly four hours. Eventually the scan was completed and a porter came with a wheelchair to return me to the ward, where I was disappointed to find a handwritten note tucked under the edge of the blanket. I knew at once from the handwriting that it was from Helen and felt completely desolated knowing that I had missed her visit. I opened the note and read that she and Jim had come for three o'clock visiting as usual and had waited until nearly seven but with no information available as to when I would get back to the ward and with a two and a half hour drive to get back home, they had made the decision to leave the hospital. The note finished by saying she would call when she got home.

I was upset, not at Helen, but just at the hopelessness of the situation. I was cold and needed the loo so I took myself off to the disabled toilet. On reflection, I'd say the colour was much more of a florescent lime green than yellow. I got back my bed, still feeing cold and shivery so I got into bed and waited for the phone call from Helen. I came to with the chap from the next bed gently shaking my shoulder; he was waking me because my phone was buzzing on the bedside cabinet. I managed to grab it in time, Helen said that she and Jim were so sorry to have missed seeing me, particularly after the news that I had been given yesterday, I said that I would tell her all about the scan when I saw her the next day.

It wasn't long before the drugs trolley arrived but before the nurse came close, I put my hand up to say stop and pointed at my new yellow bracelet. She said that she had not come across one before, so I explained to her what I had been told about being radioactive and said that she couldn't come any closer if she was pregnant. She chuckled and, with a sigh, said that chance would be a fine thing.

After she had left, but before the diazepam kicked in, I made my way back to the disabled toilet. I entered the room, locking the door behind me. With the light on, I studied my surroundings and then went across to the toilet and lifted the seat. Then, without turning round, I shuffled backwards a couple of paces towards the door until I could reach the light switch. I reached out behind me and pulled on the drop cord to turn the light off and waited a couple of seconds for my eyes to adjust to the darkness. There was just enough of a glow coming under the door from the lights in the corridor for me to be able to find my way back to the toilet. I don't know, whether this close to death, if I had reverted to having boyhood fantasies or not, but as well as it being florescent lime green, I just had to know whether it also glowed in the dark.

It was a disappointing end to a disappointing day.

Weekend – Saturday 17th and Sunday 18th December

This was the last weekend before Christmas and, if the diagnosis was correct, it could well be my last, which was a very sobering thought indeed and so I faced the day in a sombre mood. I forced myself out of bed to do battle in the washroom because, even at this late stage, I still had the need for people to remember me well and, although I was not expecting lots of people to be visiting, I knew that several friends and family would be travelling to Birmingham.

Andy arrived first, because he had come straight to the hospital from his home in Fareham and it was good to have some real time together. The different visiting arrangements at this hospital meant that he was able to stay and talk rather than be the shepherd. We chatted about family matters, past and future, and he was keen to assure me that while he would not interfere in any way, he would always support Helen and Jim as best he could.

Jim couldn't visit today because of his work, and Kate had asked me if I would mind if she didn't visit so that she could use the time to do her Christmas shopping, in preparation for her return trip to New Zealand; so I was pleased when Helen appeared at the end of the ward because I had not seen her since the previous Thursday and wanted to tell her all about what had happened during the PET scan. It made her smile when I told her about my late night antics in the loo.

Matt turned up just after lunchtime, and spelled out in some detail what had been happening with the business. He said how many of the clients had sent their condolences to me and the family and couldn't believe how suddenly this had happened to a relatively young person. Matt was obviously upset and, although brief, he managed to be business-like. I wished him luck in the future and thanked him for his pledge to protect Helen from the worry and heartache of having to deal with the business after I had gone. We shook hands and he left.

Around mid-afternoon Alan (B) and Pamela came to see me. This was the first time since I had become ill. They had driven directly up from the south coast and I was very grateful that they had made the trip because I knew what an extremely brave move it must have been on Alan's part, particularly with all the memories it would invoke for him, having suffered a near death experience himself only a year previously. Alan presented me with a book of anecdotes which he said had brought him comfort during his experience.

Visiting times at this hospital were very different to that of Hereford, so rather than an almost continuous flow of visitors coming to see me from the waiting room, two or three times over during the course of the day, it was much more a case of people arriving and leaving at set times which, on the up side, meant that there was more time in between visits for me to rest and I didn't get so tired but, on the down side, there was only one chance for anyone to say what they wanted to say and I quite often felt, after someone had left, that I should have said more.

Sunday morning brought a new emotional wrench when Andy arrived with Kate. Helen and Jim were also there, but they had driven over separately. Kate, with her bags packed and in the boot of Andy's car, ready for the off, told me that she had actually needed to buy extra suit cases to carry all of the children's Christmas presents back to New Zealand. I said that I expected that it would cost her a pretty penny in excess baggage charges. She said that it would be worth it just to see the look on their faces on Christmas morning, particularly because a lot of what she had bought was not available in New Zealand.

Kate then said, that although she had lots of photos of us all together in happier times, she would like to have one last one of us together, as we were now, to show the grandchildren when she got home, whereupon she dug around in her handbag for her camera which she handed to Andy. The three of us put on the best 'say cheese' smile we could muster, and Andy duly obliged by clicking the button. Bearing in mind where we were and the circumstances we were in, it didn't turn out to be a bad photo at all, although the NG tube gave things away a bit.

Andy had told me previously, that it would make sense for him to go straight home once he had seen Kate off on her flight, but he said that he would be back at the hospital again before the end of the week. Kate said that she needed to leave around midday, in order to catch her plane, so time was very limited on this final visit together. As it came close to the time for her and Andy to leave, it became very tearful and, after one last long lingering hug, she finally picked up her things and took a long slow walk out of the ward, dabbing at her eyes while looking at us over her shoulder. We waved a final goodbye as she disappeared round the corner and I knew that was it, I would never see her again.

It was all starting to feel very final, so I was really pleased when Alex arrived in the afternoon. She and Ian had also brought Joyce and Albert with them. However, after a while, and suffering the usual conundrum of trying to find new subjects to talk about, which is faced by all visitors of long term patients, Joyce asked me how I was getting on with the other patients, now I was in an open ward. I explained to her that my situation had not proved very conducive to making new acquaintances. In the first place I had very little voice, which made any attempt at conversing quite difficult and, once past the courtesy of an exchange of names, the next question inevitably enquired as to what ailment had landed you in hospital. I had found that telling people I had a tumour on the brain stem and that I was not likely to survive until Christmas tended to be a real conversation killer. I had therefore been polite but kept my own counsel and had not tried to strike up relationships with the other patients. She nodded her understanding and the conversation moved on.

The visiting bell tolled and my little group collected their belongings together. Each one managed to put on a brave face and said that they would try to get back to see me during the week but, above all, they hoped beyond hope, that it might come true that I would get home for a couple of days over Christmas.

As always Helen was the last to leave and, being this close to the end of our time together, every parting seemed to get harder.

Monday – 19th December

I cannot describe how it felt to wake up that Monday morning following the depressing nature of the weekend, particularly after having to say a final goodbye to Kate; I couldn't get Bob Geldof's rasping chorus of 'I Don't Like Mondays' out of my head. I couldn't be bothered to shower, or shave and, apart from the nurse's usual 'obs' round there was nothing much to do until visiting time, so having changed into a 'T' shirt and jogging bottoms, I decided to take a wander somewhere, anywhere, to try and take my mind off things.

The only walking, or rather shuffling, I had done was from my bed to the washroom and back, so I felt a bit shaky as I started out, and progress was slow but, as I ventured further afield, I gained more confidence. I realised that I had not left the confines of the ward since the previous Tuesday, apart from the times that the porter had taken me to the radiology department and I was a bit unsure which way to go; so on the virtual toss of a coin in my head I took a left at the entrance to the ward, determined to find out what lay behind the half glazed door at the end of the corridor.

I tentatively opened the door and peered around the door jamb not knowing if I might be disturbing someone. To my surprise I found an empty day room, complete with armchairs and a TV. Having satisfied my curiosity, but achieving little, I decided that I would venture further. I turned back the way I had come and having passed the Nurses' Station I found myself out in the main corridor, where I had ventured to find the public toilets on the first morning.

I made sure that I made a mental note of any landmarks along the way, so that I wouldn't get lost on the way back and, after I had been wandering pretty aimlessly, for about twenty minutes or so, I found myself at the edge of the main hospital reception area. It reminded me a bit of an airport concourse with all its modern lines and the light flooding in through the glass frontage, which did nothing to improve my mood for, as I stood there taking in all the sights and sounds, I realised that flying anywhere was something else that I would never do again; so having rested against a wall for a while I started to make my way back to the ward.

About halfway back along the main corridor, I came across an alcove with some seats and vending machines in it and, feeling drained from the effort of the walking, I decided to stop for a rest. Although I had passed this alcove on the way to the main entrance, its contents hadn't registered with me and as I looked about me I saw that one of the vending machines sold ice creams and ice lollies. I reached into my pocket and found a few coins which were left over from some money that had been given to me by Helen so that I could buy newspapers to keep myself abreast of the oil fire; I found that I had just enough for a three stage multi- coloured rocket on a stick. I stood up from the seat and fed the money into the coin slot and pressed the appropriate button, and the lolly clunked into the recess at the bottom.

I reached down for the brightly wrapped confection, which prompted memories of the times when, as a child, I had waited at an ice cream van on a warm afternoon to pay a few pence for an Orange Mivvy or a chocolate flake adorned Ninety Nine. "Strange comfort food", I thought as I removed the wrapper, but as I chewed small pieces off of it and carefully swallowed them like the fruit ice Helen had brought in for me, it felt good to do something normal again, even if was only to eat an ice lolly. However, not wanting to risk a coughing fit, I thought better of walking and eating so I continued to perch on my seat in the alcove, thoroughly enjoying the moment. The corridor was a main thoroughfare, with doctors, nurses, visitors and patients all busily moving this way and that and, as I sat there, quietly people watching, I found myself noting the colours and numbers of wrist bands that patients were wearing in comparison to my own collection; I couldn't believe I was being so competitive.

I had just about managed to get through the yellow nose cone section of the rocket without much of a struggle but I felt sure that the green and purple sections would prove to be a mission too far so, feeling suitably refreshed, I dropped the rest of the lolly into the waste bin and continued on my way back to the ward. My mood had lifted a bit after my sortie; another hump in the roller coaster of emotions I seemed to travel every day, up one minute and down the next, although hardly surprising when I thought of what was happening to me.

On my return, I texted Helen to say that she didn't have to bother with the crushed ice, because I had just eaten an ice lolly. "Well done!" came her reply text which also said that she would soon be leaving the house. So knowing that I now had a couple of hours before she arrived, I decided to make an effort after all, and went to have a shower and a shave which I completed well before she turned up, which meant that she was none the wiser about my lacklustre start to the day.

It was good to have Helen to myself after the weekend visits and, although the conversation never wandered far from the inevitable, we spent a pleasant few hours and then, having each checked that our golden cord was secured to one another, we said our goodbyes.

It had been a nothing sort of day really, just waiting for someone to let me know the outcome of the PET scan and when I would have the biopsy done, but I felt that Helen and I had managed to make the best of it and I was pleased when the phone went 'Ping!' with the arrival of a text, to let me know that she was home safe.

Tuesday – 20th December

During the morning, following the early washroom scramble, I received information, via a nurse who had attended a morning case conference that, because of the amount of non-elective surgery which was having to be fitted into the operating theatre before Christmas, the ENT surgeon, who was due to carry out my biopsy, was running out of time, and it would now probably have to be completed in the New Year.

I felt a bit guilty on hearing this news, almost as though I had cheated the hospital because, already having had the hard fought for PET scan, I might not be around long enough for them to take their pound of flesh, so to speak. However the nurse went on to say that, during the same meeting, it had been said that if my condition did not deteriorate significantly in the coming week, that there was a possibility that I could be sent home for Christmas Day and Boxing Day to enable me to have some time at home with family and friends and then return to Birmingham or more likely Hereford Hospital. This gave me a real boost; no-one had anyone actually confirmed that I might get to go home for Christmas Day before and I couldn't wait for Helen to arrive at visiting time so that I could let her know about this new development face to face; I felt that a text would not convey the same emotion.

I was sat in the chair watching the TV just prior to lunchtime, when another dietician lady came to see me. She was younger than the previous one and a bit more informal. I removed my earphones, switched the TV off and moved it out of the way. She perched on the edge of the bed and asked me how I was getting on with drinking thickened liquids. My expression probably told her all she needed to know; none the less she asked me whether I had been using the thickening agent at all and, looking floor ward, rather guiltily I shook my head. She must have evidently either been at the same case meeting this morning, or had been informed of its conclusions, because she knew that I might be going home for Christmas and she told me that it was now her challenge to get me eating pureed food so that I could at least enjoy something of my Christmas dinner.

I explained what had happed during the attempt at mousse swallowing the previous week, but she said that her colleague had already made her aware of the outcome, which made me think that this lady had probably drawn the short straw or miscalled a flipped coin in the office, for her to have been landed with this unwelcome task and I was a little surprised to see that she had not girded herself with a plastic pinny and goggles to protect herself against flying food debris. However, her positive attitude when she said that she would pop back in a minute with something to test me with, gave me the encouragement I needed to try again.

On her return I could see that she had a dish with a spoon in her hand and several sheets of kitchen roll draped over her arm, she sat back on the edge of the bed and put the dish on some kitchen roll on her lap, tucking the remaining paper into my shirt collar as a bib. The bowl contained a Weetabix biscuit that was soaking in some milk to soften it. She said that I should take a small portion of it on the spoon and put it on my tongue but, before I tried to swallow it, it was important that I should turn my chin over my left shoulder. I raised an eyebrow at this, but nevertheless carried out the instructions.

As I closed my eyes and swallowed, I half expected to pebbledash the bed covers with fragments of Weetabix; however, the food slipped down my throat almost normally and without any discomfort or reflux at all. It was a Eureka! moment. I opened my eyes and turned to look at her, I don't know whose smile was the widest. Heartened by the achievement she encouraged me to try again which I did with equal success. She explained to me that, by turning my head over my left shoulder, I was giving my one good larynx less distance to travel, so that it was more able to close off my windpipe when I swallowed, which meant that all of the food was going down to my stomach and not to my lungs.

She said for me to have another go but warned me not to take too much on the spoon at a time. After another successful swallow I asked her why someone had not told me of this technique before which would have saved me having to suffer all the nasal porridge. She shrugged her shoulders and smiled diplomatically. Taking the bowl from me, she said that I shouldn't overdo things because, having not eaten any solids for a few weeks now, my stomach would struggle to cope.

She suggested that it would be best if I continued with the NG tube for the time being and then gradually increase the amount of solid food intake over the next few days. I thanked her profusely, telling her that she had pretty much made the most positive impact on my life during the time I had been in hospital. (*On reflection, I do hope that she didn't think that I was over egging it*). Anyway, she smiled again and left with a definite spring in her step. I got the feeling that she was going back to the office to high five the first person she saw.

When Helen arrived I couldn't stop smiling as she walked towards my corner of the ward, the news of the possible home visit for Christmas and the food swallowing accomplishment just bubbled out of me. She was as excited as me with the prospect of my homecoming for Christmas. Later in the afternoon, and keen to encourage my appetite, she helped me to fill in my lunch order for the next day. It was the first time I had done so since coming into hospital and, looking down the menu, I felt confident of being able to tackle the chicken in gravy with mashed potato and mixed vegetables, although I was pretty sure that I wouldn't be able to finish it all.

Helen had already left when the tea trolley came onto the ward, so although my audience had gone, I couldn't resist having another go at swallowing something. The tea lady, who had become accustomed to bypassing my bed, was surprised when I held my hand up and requested a cup of milky tea. She placed it on the over bed table and I took some tissues to place them on my left shoulder, to protect against spillages. I then carefully lifted the cup to my lips and slowly took a sip. I held the warm liquid in my mouth for a moment, just in case I might have another extreme tea drinking session and then, before I tried to swallow, and in an effort to avoid spilling tea everywhere I placed the cup back on the over bed table. Slowly turning my head over my left shoulder, while holding the tissues in place with my right hand, I then swallowed. There was no convulsive explosion, no undignified nasal deluge, not even a drip off my chin. A result indeed. I bet that no-one else on the ward could have guessed why the bloke in the end bed, with the empty cup in his hand, had such a silly grin on his face.

As the day drew to a close I felt quite buoyed up by what I had achieved, it was something positive in a sea of negativity and to top it all, and if all went well, I might even get to go home for a couple of days to celebrate my last Christmas.

Wednesday – 21st December

This morning was the dawn of a new era for me, having been denied solid food for so long, so I got up early and elbowed my way through the wash room scrum to get washed and I was now dressed, excitedly awaiting the clatter of the breakfast trolley. I could hear it approaching and as the lady did her usual 'U' turn to bypass my bed I raised my arm and signalled that I would like her to stop. She was similarly surprised, as had been the tea lady the previous evening, when I said that I would like two Weetabix with quite a lot of milk please. This she prepared, and then placed the dish, along with a spoon, on the over bed table. I stood up and moved the chair, so that I could sit on the bed and pull the table over my knees then, by taking small spoonfuls, I managed to finish the whole lot in short order and without any mishaps. Pleased with my accomplishment, I texted Helen with the news, that I had eaten TWO Weetabix for breakfast and managed to down a cup of tea last evening. She reply texted with, "Excellent news. Well done".

For the rest of the morning I tried to busy myself with watching a bit of TV or completing a couple of puzzles in the magazine that had been brought in, but mostly my thoughts were on tasting the flavours of the hot food that would be coming on the lunch trolley. It was amazing how hospital food had taken on the character of fine dining.

Lunchtime arrived and a plate with cover and eating irons were delivered to the over bed table. The smell alone was almost satisfying enough but the thought of actually eating hot food again spurred me on and, as the dinner lady retreated, I approached the hoped for gastronomic delight, with an over inflated feeling of expectation which burst as soon as the cover was lifted.

A small portion of chicken breast lay forlornly in a puddle of thick brown liquid, which lapped at the edge of a dollop of mashed potato and mingled with a small assortment of mixed vegetables. Undeterred by this visual disappointment, I readied myself with the eating irons and, using the technique I had been shown, I managed to consume about a third of the chicken which I cut into pieces small enough to swallow whole. I also got through most of the potato and a couple of small florets of broccoli. After so long without and, although tricky to accomplish, it had proved very satisfying.

As I sat there, content with my achievement, I noticed a tall, well-built man dressed in green scrubs heading in my direction. He stopped and stood just in front of the chair and asked me if I was Mr Wilding, which I confirmed; he then reached down and took hold of my hand so that he could look at my wrist band which he then followed by asking me my date of birth.

Content that my identity was correct, he introduced himself as the ENT surgeon who had been tasked with taking the live biopsy. He flipped open the file he was carrying and pulled out a sheet. He said that he had looked at the results of the PET scan and had become concerned about carrying out the procedure for two main reasons. The first reason, he continued, was that he didn't know whether I had been made fully aware of the implications of the operation or not, but the fact was that it would need him to open up nearly half of the side of my face, in order to gain access to the site of the supposed growth and this would leave a large scar.

Open mouthed I shook my head slowly. Secondly, he went on and, more importantly, he was of the opinion that if he actually took a biopsy of the supposed growth it could well have catastrophic consequences. My stomach nearly turned over as I tried to deal with the recent consumption of food and this scary new information. With that he closed the file and said that he was going to call a further meeting about my case, to discuss the way forward, and that either he or the consultant would get back to me.

I suddenly felt that all of today's positive achievement had just been washed away. I was still sitting there, in a daze, considering this latest development, when Helen arrived. I falteringly, managed to mumble some of the details of this latest visit to her. Somewhat anxious at my demeanour, she asked me if the surgeon had said what he thought the problem was.

I realised that in my shock I had not asked him so, determined to find out, she said that she would try and get hold of someone but, before she could make a move, one of the consultant's junior doctors approached the bedside.

Helen started to ask him about the surgeon's visit but he politely stopped her and said that he was sorry but he was unable to discuss anything further at that moment. However, he had been sent to let me know that there was going to be a further case conference in the morning, at which time the consultant would be present to discuss my diagnosis. He then excused himself and left.

We were left in a state of complete confusion, nobody had given us any concrete information at all: why had the surgeon been so adamant that he did not want to perform the biopsy or the junior doctor not tell us what was to happen next? Dare we still hope that I might get home and spend some time with the family over Christmas or was it that the cancer had spread too far for the surgeon to carry out the procedure? We didn't know whether to laugh or cry.

The rest of visiting time conversation was a mixture of 'what ifs' and 'maybes' and even when Helen had left, I couldn't settle, I just hoped that when the medication came it would calm me down.

When the drugs trolley nurse arrived I told her that I had successfully managed to swallow some food during the day and that maybe I could try and swallow the tablets, but she said that it would be best if I continued to receive my medication intravenously and, after she had gone, I lay in bed with the TV drawn close, waiting for the medication to kick in and continued to watch aimlessly, until the payment card ran out.

Thursday – 22nd December

It had not been a good night, there had been so many thoughts running haywire through my brain, that even the diazepam could not relax me. Being awake early, I had been the first to the washrooms but later, when the breakfast trolley came round, I had no interest in what it had to offer and was now sat by the bed in concerned anticipation of what the day may bring, trying to work out what time the case meeting might start and when some answers would be available.

Evidently it must have been an early meeting, because around about half past nine, one of the team of junior doctors, who I had been introduced to previously, headed towards me from the entrance to the ward. I could tell, even from a distance, that there was a certain disquiet about him which fed into my own anxiety.

He greeted me in a solemn manner and then said that he had just come from the case conference and had been asked to tell me that, after a careful study of the results of the PET scan, the team could find no trace of any coalescence that would indicate a cancerous growth and therefore it had been concluded, from the more detailed information now available, that I did not have a cancer growing on my brainstem, as previously diagnosed, but rather, I had suffered from a dissection of the carotid artery and the resultant aneurysm had created pressure on the nerves where they exited the skull and, it was this that had been the cause of the paralysis from which I had been suffering.

I asked him what the team had thought might have caused the problem; he replied that it could either be a hereditary thing, or might have been a physical thing, possibly a hard sneeze or cough.

Now he had said all of this as though I should know what it all meant and seemed genuinely surprised when I looked him straight in the eye and asked whether this meant that I was still about to die or not. He replied, in a fairly perfunctory manner, that in his opinion he thought it would be unlikely.

I still wasn't sure whether I was getting the full story; the previous day I had been dying and today I'm not. Why? What had happened in the meantime to make things different? What had caused my miraculous change of circumstance and, anyway above all, why at this momentous time was I having to discuss all this with a junior doctor? Where was the consultant?

I felt the heat of anger building inside me and then I erupted. With saliva gurgling in my damaged throat, I managed to hiss at him that, if this was the case, why, for nearly a month now, had I been told that there was no hope and that I would be dead by Christmas? Didn't he understand that my wife and family had been put through hell? All the time I was animatedly using my extended right forefinger to stab at the fingers on my near useless left hand, one by one, to emphasise each point. Now with tears streaming down my face, I continued with undiminished fury, telling him how I had been forced to locate a burial plot, make a will and organise my own funeral. People had come from all over the country, in fact, from the other side of the world to say their goodbyes to me. My end of life had been organised, everything was in place. I was having a death to die for and then, just like that, he had turned up at my bedside and, in an instant, taken it all away from me.

I sat there, my chest heaved with emotional exhaustion and I coughed from the exertion on my larynx. I didn't know what he had expected, possibly my grateful thanks, but certainly not someone ranting against the news he had brought. He looked like a wide-eyed rabbit caught in a car's headlights. He wanted to get away but didn't know which way to go.

When I had calmed down a bit, I asked him what would happen next. He coughed nervously and having managed to find his voice said that, if I could arrange transport, I could go home. With that, the reality and incredulity at the enormity of the situation both hit me at the same time and I turned and buried my face in the pillow on the bed beside me and sobbed.

I felt a gentle hand on my shoulder and when I looked up I saw from across the bed the white coat of the junior doctor, as he beat a hasty retreat. I turned to see a nurse, who said sympathetically, that she would sit with me for a bit. After a while I reached for my phone. I sat there with it in my hands and just looked at it, while I tried to steel myself to make the call. The nurse, realising what I was about to do, said that she would give me some privacy and left, pulling the curtain around the bed and I dialled Helen's number.

The phone only rang once before it was answered, the first thing Helen wanted to know was had the consultant been to see me yet. In a crackling whisper I confirmed that someone had; so what had they said she asked. I put on the strongest voice I could muster and told her simply that that I wasn't going to die and that I could come home today if she wanted to pick me up. There was silence at the end of the phone and then the sound of tearful joy, followed by shouts, off phone, as she called to Jim and told him the news. Helen said that she couldn't believe it and that it was the best news ever and how she wished she was with me right now so that she could just hold me in her arms. She said that hospital visiting times could be blowed and that she would get some clothes together, jump in the car and come and get me straight away.

The phone went dead and I imagined her quickly gathering things together while trying to ring people at the same time to let them know the news. Helen's calls must have been getting through, because every so often my phone would 'Ping!' and a text offering congratulations would appear on the screen and then the phone buzzed; it was Andy ringing to hear the news for himself.

I knew that it would take at least a couple of hours for Helen to travel the distance from home and so, eager to be ready for her arrival, I started to pack away my toiletries and pulled all of the clothes out of the bedside locker so that I could fold them ready to be packed into the holdall which I knew she would bring with her. Once done, I seated myself in the chair to wait. However, I could feel my elation start to diminish; this lull now gave me time to ponder about what would happen going forward. After all I was still paralysed on my left side and I could only just make myself understood when speaking. I would not be able to drive a car myself or use the computer very well and therefore it wouldn't be possible for me to work. I hadn't taken out and critical illness insurance and so how would I pay the mortgage.

After a while the phone went 'Ping!' a text had arrived from Helen which said that she and Jim were in the car park and wouldn't be long. None of my worries could suppress the joy at seeing them as they came into the ward. By the time they got to the bedside all our faces were wet with tears. Helen dropped her cargo of my coat and the holdall and I lifted my right arm to hold her. She put both her arms around me and squeezed so hard that the cannula on the inside of my left arm dug in with a sharp pain, which made me flinch. She quickly let go and then rearranged her arms undermine, and we held each other tightly. At the same time Jim reached over Helen's shoulders so that he could also join in the clinch. After a while we slowly untied the knot of our embrace, Helen said that she could not believe that I was actually going to be walking out of the hospital with her which had been her undying prayer for the previous four weeks.

She opened the holdall and started to lay out the clothes she had brought for me to wear home; they consisted of a thick green woollen cable stitch jumper, a pair of green corduroy trousers and, as she produced some socks and a pair of shoes, I said that wearing them again would be a novelty. Jim had carried in my heavy tweed coat, a brimmed hat along with a scarf and gloves.

A senior nurse came to the bed and said how pleased she was to hear the news and that she would try to move things along as quickly as possible. However, she hoped we could understand that my sudden discharge had caught them all by surprise, which meant the relevant documents had not been prepared or signed. She went on to say that, before I could go home, I would also need to see the dietician for a pump and supplies of NG food and that a prescription would need to be signed off by a doctor so that I could take home a supply of the drugs which I had been using in hospital. This put a bit of a dampener on the proceedings and Helen asked her how long she thought it might take to which she replied that, unfortunately, because everyone would be about the hospital doing their normal work she couldn't put a time on it; however, she assured us that it would get her best attention.

Thinking that we would soon be on our way, I asked Helen to help me get dressed so that we should not be delayed any longer than was necessary. The effort of getting dressed, on top of the emotional overload of the day made me feel very tired so I sat in the chair to wait. Jim sat on the far side of the bed, somewhat disappointed to find that there was no credit left on the TV card, and Helen perched on the bed close to me and told me about all the things she planned to do over Christmas, now that I would be at home and, as we sat there talking, our happiness would sometimes spontaneously bubble over.

We didn't have to wait too long before the younger of the dieticians, who I had seen previously, came along carrying a cardboard box. She placed it on the bed beside me and asked how well I had been getting on with my swallowing. I told her that I had managed the Weetabix, also a cup of tea and a small part of the chicken dinner the previous day but that, in the excitement of that day's news, I had not tried anything else. She said that it was important that I continue to practice swallowing when I got home, at which Helen said she would make sure I did, and that she would puree all the food to make it easier for me to swallow.

The dietician then produced a pump from the box and showed us how to operate it, even though I had been using one for weeks now and suggested that, when we got home, we could use some coat hangers hung on the back of a chair, to hold the bags upright. Next she reached into the box and pulled out some sachets of the drink thickening granules, I pulled a face and she laughed and dropped them straight back in the box. We thanked her for all that she had done; she shook my hand, wished me well, smiled warmly at us both and left.

Helen said that because she had left home so quickly, she hadn't had a drink since breakfast time and was very thirsty. So while I rested in the chair, she and Jim went off in search for a drinks machine while I stayed by the bed in case anyone came. While sitting there I realised that I still had the cannula in my arm, and when the next nurse came by on her rounds, I asked her if it could be taken out. She returned with a kidney dish and removed the cannula, bathed the area and then put a plaster to cover the hole.

Helen and Jim returned with their cardboard cups of drink bringing with them an ice lolly, which they had obtained from the same machine I had found on Monday. It was very welcome as I was feeling quite warm sat there in my 'demob' clothes.

The afternoon seemed to drag on interminably, but eventually the senior nurse arrived with the discharge papers that I had to sign, which being done, she said the only outstanding item was the prescription, so she would go and see what had happened to it.

Helen and Jim must have got to the hospital at about 1.30pm, but it was nearly 6.00pm when the senior nurse finally came to us with a carrier bag full of the prescribed medications. She said that there was enough in the bag to last well after the New Year. However, as soon as possible after we got home, I should make an appointment with my GP so that I could be reinstated onto my blood pressure medication. I asked the nurse what to do if I had difficulty swallowing the tablets. She replied that I should grind them up, add some water like they did during the drugs trolley round and drink them, even if I it meant that I had to use the thickening granules to enable me to swallow the liquid.

She then removed and replaced an envelope into the bag, explaining that I should give the letter to my GP when I saw him, because it detailed the condition I had and what medication I had been taking. Then, before donning my hat and coat, I asked the senior nurse if she would mind performing one last service for me, whereupon I held out my wrist with the collection of coloured bands. She smiled and said she could understand my reluctance to wear them home, and taking a pair of scissors out of her apron pocket, she cut through all four in one go.

A porter arrived with a wheelchair, and now fully clothed, including my hat and scarf, I sat in the chair, while he pushed me towards the main entrance of the hospital. I had the cardboard box on my lap containing the NG pump and food along with the carrier bag full of tablets, while Helen walked alongside me holding my hand and Jim followed on behind carrying the holdall. The porter stopped the chair short of causing the automatic doors to open. Jim took hold of the cardboard box from my lap and I disembarked from the wheelchair, I stood there, still holding hands with Helen and looked out with trepidation at the nightscape beyond the glass frontage of the brightly lit entrance.

I pulled the scarf up over my nose, while Helen took hold of the holdall and, clasping each other's hand tightly, the three of us moved forward together. The large doors opened with a hiss and we stepped through into the cold winter air and headed in the direction of where the car was parked. We had to cross an as yet unfinished part of the car park, and the gravel crunched under our feet. I looked up at the light-polluted night sky over this Birmingham suburb at the few stars which still managed to shine through. I locked my gaze onto the brightest one and made a silent wish for continued good luck, as I took these first few steps of what, I hoped, would be many more into 'my life after death'.

NOT THE END

Epilogue

This book is a series of facts linked together in such a way as to assist the reader to make sense of them, everything you have read is true however due to the fact that we are now thirteen years on from the actual events, the time line may be slightly askew, which is not surprising considering that no-one was keeping an actual diary of events at the time.

Many people visited me while I was in both the Hereford and Birmingham hospitals however in writing this book I had to be careful not to present visiting times as a list of names and therefore I have tended to concentrate on the main characters, for this reason I apologise to anyone who feels that they have been overlooked, I can assure you that your visit was greatly appreciated at the time and has not been forgotten.

I continued to live in Herefordshire with the lovely Helen until 2014 when we retired to a bungalow in Powys.

Kate and Gary still live in New Zealand with Ruby and Ivy and eight years ago they presented us with a grandson called Harvey.

After his 'A' levels Jim went for a six week holiday to New Zealand to pick grapes and liked it so much that he stayed and has now made a home with partner Renee.

Alex and Ian have moved from Shropshire to live in Herefordshire.

Albert passed away in October 2009.

I have not sued the NHS for misdiagnosis

I no longer have a Shogun.

I would like to thank John Charles for acting as my literary mentor when writers block struck.

Life goes on.

Other books by Geoff Wilding

REPRIEVED – The continuing story, detailing what happened to Geoff and Helen following his release from hospital

Available now in Kindle and paperback versions

Nine Days in Thailand – An account of Geoff's time in Thailand following the 2004 Tsunami and his work as a health and safety consultant assisting with the International repatriation efforts

Available 2018 in Kindle and paperback versions

38482653R00119

Printed in Poland
by Amazon Fulfillment
Poland Sp. z o.o., Wrocław